TEACHER'S PET PUBLICATIONS

LITPLAN TEACHER PACK
for
Death of a Salesman
based on the play by
Arthur Miller

Written by
Mary B. Collins

© 1996 Teacher's Pet Publications
All Rights Reserved

This **LitPlan** for Arthur Miller's
Death of a Salesman
has been brought to you by Teacher's Pet Publications, Inc.

Copyright Teacher's Pet Publications 1996
11504 Hammock Point
Berlin MD 21811

Only the student materials in this unit plan
such as worksheets, study questions, assignment sheets, and tests
may be reproduced multiple times for use in the purchaser's classroom.

For any additional copyright questions,
contact Teacher's Pet Publications.

www.tpet.com

TABLE OF CONTENTS - *Death of a Salesman*

Introduction	5
Unit Objectives	8
Reading Assignment Sheet	9
Unit Outline	10
Study Questions (Short Answer)	13
Quiz/Study Questions (Multiple Choice)	23
Pre-reading Vocabulary Worksheets	41
Lesson One (Introductory Lesson)	55
Nonfiction Assignment Sheet	57
Oral Reading Evaluation Form	66
Writing Assignment 1	63
Writing Assignment 2	64
Writing Assignment 3	75
Writing Evaluation Form	78
Vocabulary Review Activities	72
Extra Writing Assignments/Discussion ?s	70
Unit Review Activities	79
Unit Tests	83
Unit Resource Materials	115
Vocabulary Resource Materials	129

A FEW NOTES ABOUT THE AUTHOR
ARTHUR MILLER

Mr. Miller was born in Harlem (New York) on October 17, 1915. He attended public schools, but quit before graduation. He held odd jobs such as farmhand, laborer, etc. Later, he got into The University of Michigan where he wrote and attended classes. In 1938 he graduated from The University of Michigan.

In 1949 Mr. Miller won the Pulitzer Prize for *Death of a Salesman*. In 1953 *The Crucible* was produced on Broadway. Other notable works by Arthur Miller include *All My Sons, After The Fall, A View From The Bridge, The Price, Incident at Vichy,* and *The Misfits* (a movie starring Marilyn Monroe, to whom he was once married.)

--- Courtesy of Compton's Learning Company

INTRODUCTION

This unit has been designed to develop students' reading, writing, thinking, and language skills through exercises and activities related to *Death of a Salesman* by Arthur Miller. It includes nineteen lessons, supported by extra resource materials.

The **introductory lesson** introduces students to one main idea in the play through a bulletin board activity. Following the introductory activity, students are given a transition to explain how the activity relates to the book they are about to read. Following the transition, students are given the materials they will be using during the unit. At the end of the lesson, students begin the pre-reading work for the first reading assignment.

The **reading assignments** are approximately thirty pages each; some are a little shorter while others are a little longer. Students have approximately 15 minutes of pre-reading work to do prior to each reading assignment. This pre-reading work involves reviewing the study questions for the assignment and doing some vocabulary work for 8 to 10 vocabulary words they will encounter in their reading.

The **study guide questions** are fact-based questions; students can find the answers to these questions right in the text. These questions come in two formats: short answer or multiple choice. The best use of these materials is probably to use the short answer version of the questions as study guides for students (since answers will be more complete), and to use the multiple choice version for occasional quizzes. If your school has the appropriate equipment, it might be a good idea to make transparencies of your answer keys for the overhead projector.

The **vocabulary work** is intended to enrich students' vocabularies as well as to aid in the students' understanding of the book. Prior to each reading assignment, students will complete a two-part worksheet for approximately 8 to 10 vocabulary words in the upcoming reading assignment. Part I focuses on students' use of general knowledge and contextual clues by giving the sentence in which the word appears in the text. Students are then to write down what they think the words mean based on the words' usage. Part II nails down the definitions of the words by giving students dictionary definitions of the words and having students match the words to the correct definitions based on the words' contextual usage. Students should then have an understanding of the words when they meet them in the text.

After each reading assignment, students will go back and formulate answers for the study guide questions. Discussion of these questions serves as a **review** of the most important events and ideas presented in the reading assignments.

After students complete reading the work, a lesson is devoted to the **extra discussion questions/writing assignments**. These questions focus on interpretation, critical analysis and personal response, employing a variety of thinking skills and adding to the students' understanding of the play.

Following the discussion, there is a **vocabulary review** lesson which pulls together all of the fragmented vocabulary lists for the reading assignments and gives students a review of all of the words they have studied.

The **group activity** which follows the discussion questions has students working in small groups to discuss the main themes of the play. Using the information they have acquired so far through individual work and class discussions, students get together to further examine the text and to brainstorm ideas relating to the themes of the play.

The group activity is followed by a **reports and discussion** session in which the groups share their ideas about the themes with the entire class; thus, the entire class is exposed to information about all of the themes and the entire class can discuss each theme based on the nucleus of information brought forth by each of the groups.

There are three **writing assignments** in this unit, each with the purpose of informing, persuading, or having students express personal opinions. The first assignment is to inform: students create a sales plan relating to the class project. The second assignment is to persuade: students write a sales speech in which they convince someone to buy their products. The third assignment is to give students a chance to express their own opinions: students evaluate the success of the class project and tell about their own experiences with it.

In addition, there is a **nonfiction reading assignment**. Students are required to read a piece of nonfiction related in some way to *Death of a Salesman*. After reading their nonfiction pieces, students will fill out a worksheet on which they answer questions regarding facts, interpretation, criticism, and personal opinions. During one class period, students make **oral presentations** about the nonfiction pieces they have read. This not only exposes all students to a wealth of information, it also gives students the opportunity to practice **public speaking**.

The **review lesson** pulls together all of the aspects of the unit. The teacher is given four or five choices of activities or games to use which all serve the same basic function of reviewing all of the information presented in the unit.

The **unit test** comes in two formats: short answer or multiple choice. As a convenience, two different tests for each format have been included. There is also an advanced short answer unit test for higher level students.

There are additional **support materials** included with this unit. The **extra activities packet** includes suggestions for an in-class library, crossword and word search puzzles related to the play, and extra vocabulary worksheets. There is a list of **bulletin board ideas** which gives the teacher suggestions for bulletin boards to go along with this unit. In addition, there is a list of **extra class activities** the teacher could choose from to enhance the unit or as a substitution for an exercise the teacher might feel is inappropriate for his/her class. **Answer keys** are located directly after the **reproducible student materials** throughout the unit. The student materials may be reproduced for use in the teacher's classroom without infringement of copyrights. No other portion of this unit may be reproduced without the written consent of Teacher's Pet Publications, Inc.

The **level** of this unit can be varied depending upon the criteria on which the individual assignments are graded, the teacher's expectations of his/her students in class discussions, and the formats chosen for the study guides, quizzes and test. If teachers have other ideas/activities they wish to use, they can usually easily be inserted prior to the review lesson.

UNIT OBJECTIVES - *Death of a Salesman*

1. Through reading Arthur Miller's Death of a Salesman, students will gain a better understanding of the importance of one's own values.

2. Students will demonstrate their understanding of the text on four levels: factual, interpretive, critical and personal.

3. Students will actually become salespeople in the class project related to this unit.

4. Students will study the symbolism in the play and look at the theme of reality versus illusion.

5. Students will look at advertisements to see how they affect us in our daily lives.

6. Students will be given the opportunity to practice reading aloud and silently to improve their skills in each area.

7. Students will answer questions to demonstrate their knowledge and understanding of the main events and characters in *Death of a Salesman* as they relate to the author's theme development.

8. Students will enrich their vocabularies and improve their understanding of the play through the vocabulary lessons prepared for use in conjunction with the play.

9. The writing assignments in this unit are geared to several purposes:
    a. To have students demonstrate their abilities to inform, to persuade, or to express their own personal ideas
        Note: Students will demonstrate ability to write effectively to <u>inform</u> by developing and organizing facts to convey information. Students will demonstrate the ability to write effectively to <u>persuade</u> by selecting and organizing relevant information, establishing an argumentative purpose, and by designing an appropriate strategy for an identified audience. Students will demonstrate the ability to write effectively to <u>express personal ideas</u> by selecting a form and its appropriate elements.
    b. To check the students' reading comprehension
    c. To make students think about the ideas presented by the play
    d. To encourage logical thinking
    e. To provide an opportunity to practice good grammar and improve students' use of the English language.

10. Students will read aloud, report, and participate in large and small group discussions to improve their public speaking and personal interaction skills.

READING ASSIGNMENT SHEET - *Death of a Salesman*

Date Assigned	RA#	Section Assigned	Completion Date
	1	Beginning of Act One to the woman's appearance	
	2	The woman's appearance to the end of Act One	
	3	Beginning of Act Two to Charley's 2nd entrance	
	4	Charley's 2nd entrance to end of the restaurant scene	
	5	End of the restaurant scene to end of the play	

UNIT OUTLINE - *Death of a Salesman*

1 Introduction	2 Speaker	3 Project Work	4 Writing Assignment #1	5 Writing Assignment #2 PV RA 1
6 Read RA 1 PV RA 2	7 Study ?s RA 1 Read RA 2 PV RA 3	8 Study ?s RA 2 Read RA 3 PV RA 4	9 Study ?s RA 3 Read RA 4 PV RA 5	10 Study ?s RA 4 Read RA 5
11 Study ?s RA 5 Extra Discussion ?s	12 Vocabulary	13 Group Activity	14 Reports & Discussion	15 Library
16 Writing Assignment #3	17 NFR Reports	18 Review & Writing Conferences	19 Test	

Key: P = Preview Study Questions   V = Prereading Vocabulary Worksheets   RA = Reading Assignment

STUDY GUIDE QUESTIONS

SHORT ANSWER STUDY GUIDE QUESTIONS - *Death of a Salesman*

Act One

1. Who is Willy Loman?
2. Identify Linda.
3. What happened to Willy after he got a little above Yonkers?
4. What is Linda's reaction to Willy's complaints about himself?
5. What reason does Willy give that he can't work in New York?
6. Identify Biff and Happy.
7. In the first scene with Linda, Willy contradicted himself twice. About what did he contradict himself?
8. What seems to be the problem between Biff and Willy?
9. Why doesn't Happy go west with Biff?
10. What does Biff want from Bill Oliver?
11. Why did Biff stop working for Bill Oliver?
12. Happy says, "I don't know what to do about him [Willy], it's getting embarrassing." To what is he referring, and what does the fact that Happy thinks this way tell you about his character?
13. Why does Willy talk so much about the car?
14. Where did Biff get the football? What does Willy say about that?
15. What does Willy admit to Linda about his business? What is her reaction?
16. Who is The Woman?
17. What does Willy mean, "I'll make it up to you, Linda, I'll --"? What does Linda think he means?
18. What does Willy want young Bernard to do for Biff?
19. What does Willy tell Happy about Ben when Happy asks how Ben "did it"?
20. Who is Ben?
21. Who is Charley?
22. Charley says, "To hell with it. When a deposit bottle is broken, you don't get your nickel back." What does he mean?
23. Charley and Willy are playing cards. Why does Charley leave?
24. What did Willy's father do for a living? How is that different from what Willy does?
25. Why does Charley tell Willy "the jails are full of fearless characters"?
26. Linda says, "Attention, attention must be paid to such a person." Explain.
27. Linda tells the boys that Willy won't be all right. When the boys ask why he won't, what is her reply?
28. What advice does Willy give Biff on the evening before he goes to see Bill Oliver? How does Willy contradict himself again?
29. How much time passes in the first act? How much time are we given information about?

Short Answer Study Guide Questions - *Death of a Salesman* - Page Two

Act Two
1. Where did Biff go early that morning?
2. What did Willy resolve to talk about with Howard?
3. What is the result of Willy's conversation with Howard?
4. "You can't eat the orange and throw the peel away -- a man isn't a piece of fruit!" Explain why Willy said that.
5. "This is no time for false pride, Willy. . . . You've got two great boys, haven't you?" What is sadly ironic about this statement?
6. Why didn't Willy go with Ben years ago when Ben offered him a job?
7. Ben says. "What are you building? Lay your hands on it. Where is it?" What is the point of this line?
8. Where does Willy go after his conversation with Howard?
9. What does Willy ask Bernard?
10. What was Bernard's reply?
11. Why can't Willy work for Charley?
12. Biff says, ". . . I realized what a ridiculous lie my whole life has been." What does he mean?
13. What was the result of Biff's meeting with Bill Oliver?
14. What does Happy want Biff to tell Willy?
15. Willy says, ". . . the woods are burning, boys. Can't you understand? There's a big blaze going on all around." What does that mean?
16. What does Willy do while Biff is trying to explain the facts of his meeting with Bill Oliver?
17. What did Biff take from Bill Oliver?
18. Identify Miss Forsythe and Letta.
19. Where does Willy go?
20. What is Biff's opinion of his father now, when he tells it to Miss Forsythe?
21. Why can't Biff help Willy?
22. Happy denies that Willy is his father. Why?
23. What happened in Boston? What do we finally find out is the problem, the secret between Willy and Biff?
24. Why did Biff go to Boston in the first place?
25. Where does Willy go after he realizes that the boys have left him at the restaurant?
26. Why does Linda knock the flowers to the floor?
27. Willy says, "A man can't go out the way he came in, Ben, a man has got to add up to something." What does he mean?

Short Answer Study Guide Questions - *Death of a Salesman* - Page Three

28. Why does Willy decide to kill himself?
29. What does Biff want to tell Willy before he is ready to go?
30. Biff says, "Will you take that phony dream and burn it before something happens?" What is the significance of this line?
31. What is Willy's response to Biff's whole scene when Biff ends up crying?
32. Ben says, "The jungle is dark but full of diamonds, Willy." Explain.
33. What does Willy do?
34. Why is the car an appropriate device?
35. Biff says, "He had all the wrong dreams. All, all wrong." Explain.
36. Based on the events of the play and our knowledge of the characters, what will probably become of Biff and Happy?
37. Linda says, "We're free and clear." What is the double meaning here?

ANSWER KEY SHORT ANSWER STUDY GUIDE QUESTIONS - *Death of a Salesman*

<u>Act One</u>

1. Who is Willy Loman?
    Willy is a salesman who, after thirty-four years with the company, has been taken off salary and is experiencing some personal and financial difficulties.

2. Identify Linda.
    Linda is Willy's wife.

3. What happened to Willy after he got a little above Yonkers?
    He forgot he was driving and ran off of the road. His daydreams took the place of his reality for a short time, and he nearly had an accident.

4. What is Linda's reaction to Willy's complaints about himself?
    Linda makes excuses for him.

5. What reason does Willy give that he can't work in New York?
    He is the New England man. He is vital to New England.

6. Identify Biff and Happy.
    Biff and Happy are the Lomans' boys. Biff is the older of the two and is very unsettled. Happy has largely been ignored as the two were growing up, and, as his name suggests, is happy-go-lucky without being very responsible.

7. In the first scene with Linda, Willy contradicted himself twice. About what did he contradict himself?
    First, Willy calls Biff lazy, but later he describes him as hard-working. Willy also contradicts himself about the windshield of the car.

8. What seems to be the problem between Biff and Willy?
    They apparently never got along when Biff lived at home. Also, Biff is unsettled and hasn't made anything of himself yet, and this distresses Willy.

9. Why doesn't Happy go west with Biff?
    He wants to "show some of those pompous, self-important executives over there that Hap Loman can make the grade."

10. What does Biff want from Bill Oliver?
    Biff wants money to buy a ranch.

11. Why did Biff stop working for Bill Oliver?
    He suspected Oliver knew he had stolen some basketballs.

12. Happy says, "I don't know what to do about him [Willy], it's getting embarrassing." To what is he referring, and what does the fact that Happy thinks this way tell you about his character?

    He is referring to Willy's mental lapses into a dream world, his forgetfulness. Happy doesn't express particular concern for Willy; rather, he is concerned about being embarrassed in public with Willy.

13. Why does Willy talk so much about the car?

    Willy has had a bad experience in his car today, and the old car is a happy experience from the past. Being a traveling salesman, Willy's car would be very important to him. It is almost symbolic of his way of life -- now his deteriorating way of life.

14. Where did Biff get the football? What does Willy say about that?

    Biff had stolen it from school. Willy said that the coach would probably congratulate him for his industriousness.

15. What does Willy admit to Linda about his business? What is her reaction?

    He tells her that business isn't so good, that people don't seem to like him. Linda makes excuses for him.

16. Who is The Woman?

    The Woman is someone Willy apparently had a not-very-meaningful affair with while he was away on business at some time.

17. What does Willy mean, "I'll make it up to you, Linda, I'll --"? What does Linda think he means?

    Willy means that he'll make up for his infidelity. Linda thinks he is still talking about his business and will try to make more money for them.

18. What does Willy want young Bernard to do for Biff?

    Willy wants Bernard to give Biff answers for a test.

19. What does Willy tell Happy about Ben when Happy asks how Ben "did it"?

    He said, ". . . The man knew what he wanted and went out and got it! Walked into a jungle, and comes out, the age of twenty-one, and he's rich. The world is an oyster, but you don't crack it open on a mattress!"

20. Who is Ben?

    Ben is Willy's brother who apparently became very successful at a young age.

21. Who is Charley?

    Charley is a long-time friend of Willy (although Willy doesn't really think of Charley as a friend until near the end of the play).

22. Charley says, "To hell with it. When a deposit bottle is broken, you don't get your nickel back." What does he mean?
    One may invest a lot of time and money into a child, but if the child doesn't turn out well, you won't get any satisfaction or rewards for your time spent. But, there's no use worrying about it; you just pick up and go on with your own life, and let it go.

23. Charley and Willy are playing cards. Why does Charley leave?
    Willy is, besides being rude to him, not making any sense since he is talking to imaginary Ben at the same time he is talking to real Charley.

24. What did Willy's father do for a living? How is that different from what Willy does?
    Willy's father made flutes and traveled from town to town selling them. Willy doesn't have the pride of craftsmanship that Mr. Loman had; Willy sells someone else's product and just plays a personality game to try to get sales.

25. Why does Charley tell Willy "the jails are full of fearless characters"?
    Willy had just sent his boys across the road to a new construction site to steal more building supplies. Willy is proud of their fearlessness, but Charley sees a more practical side to it, that what the boys are doing is wrong.

26. Linda says, "Attention, attention must be paid to such a person." Explain.
    However misguided Willy is, he is still a person trying to muddle through life as well as he can, and he deserves our attention, our interest and caring, to try to help him make it through as much as we can.

27. Linda tells the boys that Willy won't be all right. When the boys ask why he won't, what is her reply?
    She tells them that Willy is trying to kill himself.

28. What advice does Willy give Biff on the evening before he goes to see Bill Oliver? How does Willy contradict himself again?
    Wear a business suit, talk as little as possible, don't make jokes, walk in seriously, ask for fifteen thousand dollars, don't say, "Gee," walk in with a big laugh and tell a couple of stories to lighten things up, and that personality wins the day. The contradictions are that Biff is not supposed to talk much, but he is supposed to start out with a couple of stories. He is to be serious and not joke, yet he is supposed to "lighten things up."

29. How much time passes in the first act? How much time are we given information about?
    Only a day passes in Act I, but we are given information about the family from the time the children were small.

Act Two

1. Where did Biff go early that morning?
   Biff went to see Mr. Oliver.

2. What did Willy resolve to talk about with Howard?
   He would talk to Howard about the New York job.

3. What is the result of Willy's conversation with Howard?
   Willy is essentially fired.

4. "You can't eat the orange and throw the peel away -- a man isn't a piece of fruit!" Explain why Willy said that.
   Willy had spent the best years of his life working for the company, and now in his old age, they are letting him go since there is no more use for him.

5. "This is no time for false pride, Willy. . . . You've got two great boys, haven't you?" What is sadly ironic about this statement?
   It is true; this _is_ no time for false pride; however, Willy has had such false pride all through his life that he has made the boys out to be more than they are. Now when he really does need the boys, the reality of their worthlessness crushes Willy's idealized version, and Willy is in a catch-22, no win situation.

6. Why didn't Willy go with Ben years ago when Ben offered him a job?
   He had inflated his own business worth to Linda, so that when the opportunity came to go with Ben, Linda didn't see the need since Willy was on such a great career path.

7. Ben says. "What are you building? Lay your hands on it. Where is it?" What is the point of this line?
   In fact, Willy can't put his hands on anything worthwhile he has made in his life. He is always in debt, he is a failure at business, and his boys appear to be just like him.

8. Where does Willy go after his conversation with Howard?
   He goes to see Charley for money to cover his life insurance premium payment.

9. What does Willy ask Bernard?
   He wants to know if Bernard understands what went wrong with Biff, why Biff did not do anything with his life after the age of 17.

10. What was Bernard's reply?
    Biff was ready to go to summer school to make up the math class, but when he returned from Boston, he gave up. Bernard figured out that something must have happened in Boston.

11. Why can't Willy work for Charley?
    Charley stands for the things Willy does not believe in; if Willy would work for Charley, he would admit that his whole life had been wrong.

12. Biff says, ". . . I realized what a ridiculous lie my whole life has been." What does he mean?
    Biff finally realized that he was raised on a false philosophy and that most of the things that happened were glossed over and made far better than they were. The glossy versions of things were repeated so often that even the participants had believed they were true. Taking away all of the gloss, Biff realized that he was a clerk and a thief.

13. What was the result of Biff's meeting with Bill Oliver?
    Basically, he got brushed aside. He would not ever get the money, and he would have no more meetings with Bill Oliver.

14. What does Happy want Biff to tell Willy?
    He wants Biff to tell Willy that there will be another meeting with Bill Oliver. Happy wants Biff to paint a glossy picture for Willy instead of telling him the truth.

15. Willy says, ". . . the woods are burning, boys. Can't you understand? There's a big blaze going on all around." What does that mean?
    Willy's world is falling apart. He has lost his job and has no resources. He is getting trapped by the years of lies he has lived.

16. What does Willy do while Biff is trying to explain the facts of his meeting with Bill Oliver?
    Willy daydreams about the time Biff flunked math.

17. What did Biff take from Bill Oliver?
    Biff took Bill Oliver's fountain pen.

18. Identify Miss Forsythe and Letta.
    They are women who come into the restaurant. Happy is more interested in getting a date with them than in the welfare of his own father.

19. Where does Willy go?
    Willy goes to the restroom to compose himself.

20. What is Biff's opinion of his father now, when he tells it to Miss Forsythe?
    He calls his father a "fine, troubled prince."

21. Why can't Biff help Willy?
    He can't help Willy because they don't communicate well. They both just get frustrated and yell at each other.

22. Happy denies that Willy is his father. Why?
    Happy is embarrassed by Willy, and he does not want the responsibility of caring for Willy. After all, Happy never has had much attention from Willy, either. Everything Willy does is for Biff.

23. What happened in Boston? What do we finally find out is the problem, the secret between Willy and Biff?
    When he was 17, Biff went to Boston to talk to his father. When he got there, he walked in on his father and the woman with whom he had an affair.

24. Why did Biff go to Boston in the first place?
    He went to get his father to talk to the teachers at school to try to get his grade changed. He thought his father's personality could help him not have to go to summer school.

25. Where does Willy go after he realizes that the boys have left him at the restaurant?
    He goes and buys some carrot seeds and goes home to plant them in his garden.

26. Why does Linda knock the flowers to the floor?
    She is furious because the boys left Willy at the restaurant.

27. Willy says, "A man can't go out the way he came in, Ben, a man has got to add up to something." What does he mean?
    Willy can't see any worth in his life. He feels like he ought to have contributed something to the world, to have something to leave his mark on the world.

28. Why does Willy decide to kill himself?
    By killing himself so that it looks like an accident, Willy can leave Biff a lot of insurance money. By leaving the money, he has left something in the world. Also, Willy probably thinks that Biff will make something of himself if he has the money, thereby Willy has left a successful person behind as well.

29. What does Biff want to tell Willy before he is ready to go?
    He wants to tell Willy that he (Biff) is nothing, that he accepts that now, and that he has no hard feelings towards Willy.

30. Biff says, "Will you take that phony dream and burn it before something happens?" What is the significance of this line?
    Biff realizes that Willy's philosophy is false and that no good will come of it. This line foreshadows Willy's death, and it brings together the dream/illusion motif with the "woods are burning" motif.

31. What is Willy's response to Biff's whole scene when Biff ends up crying?
    He says, "Isn't that -- isn't that remarkable? Biff -- he likes me!"

32. Ben says, "The jungle is dark but full of diamonds, Willy." Explain.
    The jungle is death. The diamonds represent the insurance money.

33. What does Willy do?
    He speeds away in his car and has a fatal car accident.

34. Why is the car an appropriate device?
    The car could symbolize his life as a traveling salesman, and his philosophy for success in life in general. It is appropriate that the car, as such a symbol, would be the means to his end.

35. Biff says, "He had all the wrong dreams. All, all wrong." Explain.
    Biff realized that Willy's philosophy was wrong, and he realized that most of Willy's life was made up of illusions.

36. Based on the events of the play and our knowledge of the characters, what will probably become of Biff and Happy?
    Biff will probably become a productive citizen in a realistic world. Happy will probably follow more in Willy's footsteps.

37. Linda says, "We're free and clear." What is the double meaning here?
    It is ironic that just at the time when Willy dies, the mortgage is paid on their home. Willy would have owned something tangible even if he hadn't used the insurance policy. Willy and Linda would have been more financially free. Also, now that Willy is dead, he is free of the conflicts presented by his philosophy; although he is literally boxed in, he is free of worldly concerns. Biff is free of Willy's influence (and ironically, probably would have been even if Willy hadn't died).

MULTIPLE CHOICE STUDY GUIDE/QUIZ QUESTIONS - *Death of a Salesman*

Act One

1. The main character is a salesman who, after thirty four years with the company, has been taken off salary and is experiencing some personal and financial difficulties. What is his name?
    a. His name is Willy Loman
    b. His name is Charley Wills.
    c. His name is Ben Happs.
    d. His name is William Benson.

2. Who is Willy's wife?
    a. Her name is Jenny.
    b. Her name is Letty.
    c. Her name is Linda.
    d. Her name is Happy.

3. What happened to Willy after he got a little above Yonkers?
    a. He ran out of gas.
    b. He forgot he was driving and ran off the road.
    c. He ran into a truck.
    d. He had a heart attack while driving.

4. What is Linda's reaction to Willy's complaints about himself?
    a. She agrees and says she never should have married him.
    b. She urges him to see a therapist.
    c. She cries and says not to talk like that.
    d. She makes excuses for him.

5. What reason does Willy give that he can't work in New York?
    a. He would not be able to find work.
    b. He is the New England man.
    c. He is vital to New England.
    d. b & c

6. Who are Biff and Happy?
    a. They are two new young salesmen who are trying to get Willy's territory.
    b. They are Willy's sons. Neither are very settled or responsible.
    c. They are Willy's older brothers. They are both highly successful, and ridicule Willy for his failure.
    d. They are two neighbors. Willy owes them both money.

Multiple Choice Study Guide Questions - *Death of a Salesman* - Page Two

7. In the first scene with Linda, Willy contradicted himself twice. About what did he contradict himself?
    a. He called Biff lazy, but later describes him as hardworking. Later he contradicts himself about the windshield of the car.
    b. He says Ben made in his money in oil, but later says real estate. He says he remembers his boys' birthdays, but later admits that he doesn't.
    c. First he says he doesn't love Linda, then he says he never said that. Then he says he had one accident, although he know he has had three.
    d. He says he wants to retire, then says he wants to work for ten more years. Then he says Happy is his favorite son, although he later tells Biff he is the favorite.

8. What seems to be the problem between Biff and Willy?
    a. Biff is a draft dodger, and Willy wanted him to have a military career.
    b. Biff was disrespectful to his mother, and Wily was angry about it.
    c. Biff wants to move to Alaska, but Willy wants him to go into sales and take over his (Willy's) route.
    d. Biff is unsettled and hasn't made anything of himself yet, and this distress Willy.

9. Why doesn't Happy go west with Biff?
    a. He is about to be married, and his wife-to-be won't let him go.
    b. He has just applied to graduate school.
    c. He wants to show the executives in his company that he can make the grade.
    d. He is too insecure to try something that risky.

10. What does Biff want from Bill Oliver?
    a. He wants money to buy a ranch.
    b. He wants a recommendation to a film director Bill knows in Hollywood.
    c. He wants his old job back.
    d. Biff wants Bill Oliver to become partners with him and open a consulting service.

11. Why did Biff stop working for Bill Oliver?
    a. Bill never gave him a raise in four years.
    b. Biff suspected Bill knew he had stolen some basketballs.
    c. Biff had been dating Bill's daughter; Bill fired him when Biff dropped her.
    d. Bill wanted Biff to lie to an insurance adjuster, and Biff refused.

Multiple Choice Study Guide Questions - *Death of a Salesman* - Page Three

12. Happy says, "I don't know what to do about him [Willy], it's getting embarrassing." What is he referring to?
    a. He is referring to Willy's growing obesity.
    b. He is referring to Willy's crude gestures and language.
    c. He is referring to Willy's excessive spending.
    d. He is referring to Willy's mental lapses into a dream world.

13. What does Happy's thinking tell you about his character?
    a. It shows that Happy really loves Willy.
    b. It shows that Happy is more concerned about his own welfare than Willy's health.
    c. Happy is admitting his ignorance, and acknowledging that he should have studied more in school.
    d. Happy prefers his mother to his father.

14. Why does Willy talk so much about the car?
    a. Buying a new car for his wife is his motivation for keeping his sales job.
    b. He thinks the car makes him seem powerful.
    c. He had a bad experience in his car today, and the old car is a happy experience from the past.
    d. He has developed a nervous phobia, and thinks that talking about he car will bring him good luck. Not talking about it may bring bad luck.

15. Where did Biff get the football?
    a. Biff had stolen it from school.
    b. Biff had received it as a gift from his mother.
    c. He borrowed it from Happy
    d. He had stolen it from a kid down the street

16. What does Willy tell Linda about his business?
    a. He's doing great and should get a promotion in a few weeks.
    b. Business isn't so good.
    c. People he does business with don't seem to like him.
    d. B & C

17. Who is The Woman?
    a. Linda
    b. Someone with whom Willy and a brief affair
    c. Willy's best client
    d. Ben's wife

Multiple Choice Study Guide Questions - *Death of a Salesman* - Page Four

18. What does Willy mean, "I'll make it up to you, Linda, I'll --"? What does Linda think he means?
    a. Willy means that he'll make up for his infidelity, Linda thinks he is talking about his business and will try to make more money for them.
    b. Willy means that he will pay more attention to her when he's home. She is thinking the same thing.
    c. Willy means he will make more money, Linda thinks he is talking about spending more time together.
    d. Willy means he'll spend more time with her and the boys. Linda thinks he is talking about his past indiscretions.

19. What does Willy want young Bernard to do for Biff?
    a. Willy wants Bernard to give up his position on the football team so that Biff can get on it.
    b. Willy wants Bernard to give Biff answers for a test.
    c. Willy wants Bernard to introduce Biff to his (Bernard's) sister, whom Biff likes.
    d. Willy wants Bernard to beat up a bully who has been bothering Biff.

20. Willy says, "The man knew what he wanted and went out and got it! Walked into a jungle, and comes out, at the age of twenty one, and he rich..." About whom it he talking?
    a. He is talking about Happy.
    b. He is talking about himself.
    c. He is talking about Ben.
    d. He is talking about Charley.

21. Who is Ben?
    a. He is Willy's brother who apparently became very successful at a young age.
    b. He is Willy's father, who was also a salesman.
    c. He is Willy's long time friend.
    d. He is Willy's oldest son, who no longer keeps in touch with the family.

22. Who is Charley?
    a. Willy's other brother
    b. A long-time friend of Willy
    c. Willy's boss
    d. Biff's real father

Multiple Choice Study Guide Questions - *Death of a Salesman* - Page Five

23. Charley says, "To hell with it. When a deposit bottle is broken, you don't get your nickel back." What does he mean?
    a. One may invest a lot of time and money into a child, but if the child doesn't turn out well, you won't get any satisfaction or rewards for your time spent. But, there's no use worrying about it; you just pick up and go on with your life.
    b. He's explaining to a client that he cannot accept returns for broken goods.
    c. If you don't live a good life, you won't have any rewards at the end of your life. In order to get to heaven, you have to be good on Earth.
    d. He is tired of listening to Willy whine about all that has gone wrong in his life, and he's just trying to cut him off short so he doesn't have to listen to him anymore.

24. Charley and Willy are playing cards. Why does Charley leave?
    a. Willy is being rude to him and not making any sense.
    b. He has another appointment to go to.
    c. He's just tired.
    d. Willy and Ben have won all of his money, so he has to quit.

25. How is what Willy's father did for a living different from what Willy does?
    a. Willy's father was a teacher. He traveled to teach short courses in different areas.
    b. Willy's father made flutes and sold them. Willy sells someone else's product and doesn't have the pride of craftsmanship that his father did.
    c. Willy's father was uneducated, and was never able to advance. Willy has a degree in business, although he had chosen not to make good use of it.
    d. Willy's father was an intellectual and an inventor. He had brilliant ideas but was never able to make a profit with them. Willy never though much about ideas; instead, he concentrated on making money.

26. Why does Charley tell Willy "the jails are full of fearless characters"?
    a. There has been a series of burglaries in their neighborhood. They have been discussing ways to scare away the young hoodlums.
    b. Charley's son has recently been sentenced to five years in jail for armed robbery. Charley is saving face, pretending he is not afraid for his son's safety in prison.
    c. Willy has just sent his sons across the road to a new construction site to steal more building supplies. Willy is proud of their fearlessness, but Charley sees a more practical side to it, that what the boys are doing is wrong.
    d. Willy has shared a rather shady business scheme with Charley. Charley doesn't want to participate, and Willy calls him a coward.

Multiple Choice Study Guide Questions - *Death of a Salesman* - Page Six

27. Linda says, "Attention, attention must be paid to such a person." Explain.
    a. Willy deserves our attention, our interest, and caring. Even though he is misguided, he is trying to muddle through life as well as he can.
    b. Biff is having a difficult time, and his parents should help him instead of criticizing.
    c. They would all do well to study Ben's methods for success and copy them.
    d. She thinks Charley is dangerous, and wants Willy to stop talking to him. She cites several instances that happened while Willy was away, Willy disagrees with his wife.

28. Linda tells the boys that Willy won't be all right. When the boys ask why he won't, what is her reply?
    a. He is dying of cancer.
    b. A psychiatrist has suggested that he go into a hospital for observation.
    c. He is trying to kill himself.
    d. She is planning to leave him, and her departure will be very difficult for him.

29. What advice does Willy give Biff on the evening before he goes to see Bill Oliver? Three of the following sentences repeat some of the advice. Which does not?
    a. Wear a business suit.
    b. Ask for fifteen thousand dollars.
    c. Walk in seriously.
    d. Carry a leather briefcase.

30. How much time passes in the first act?
    a. One day passes.
    b. Ten years pass.
    c. Two weeks pass.
    d. Three hours pass.

31. How much time are we given information about?
    a. We are given information about three years.
    b. We are given information about eight years.
    c. We are given information about the family from the time the children are small.
    d. We are given information about the last few hours before Willy's death.

Multiple Choice Study Guide Questions - *Death of a Salesman* - Page Seven

Act Two
1. Where did Biff go early that morning?
    a. He went to see Willy's boss.
    b. He went to see Mr. Oliver.
    c. He went to see The Woman
    d. He went to see Charley.

2. What did Willy resolve to talk about with Howard?
    a. He resolved to talk about old times.
    b. He resolved to talk about his family.
    c. He resolved to talk about his past successes.
    d. He resolved to talk about the New York job.

3. What is the result of Willy's conversation with Howard?
    a. Willy is fired.
    b. Willy gets the New York job.
    c. Willy quits.
    d. Willy keeps his present territory.

35. "You can't eat the orange and throw the peel away -- a man isn't a piece of fruit!" Explain why Willy said that.
    a. He is trying to convince his family he isn't crazy - "a fruitcake."
    b. He is telling his family they have to accept him the way he is, and never expect to be rich.
    c. He has spent the best years of his life working for the company, and now, in his old age, they are letting him go since there is no use for him.
    d. He finally realizes that he has to accept his own shortcomings as well as his son Biff's.

5. "This is no time for false pride, Willy. . . . You've got two great boys, haven't you?" Now that Willy really needs the boys, the reality of their worthlessness crushes his idealized version, and Willy is in a Catch-22, no win situation. Which literary element is being used here?
    a. This is a rhetorical question.
    b. This is foreshadowing.
    c. This is figurative language.
    d. This is irony.

Multiple Choice Study Guide Questions - *Death of a Salesman* - Page Eight

6. Why didn't Willy go with Ben years ago when Ben offered him a job?
    a. He wanted to make it on his own.
    b. He had inflated his own business worth to Linda, so that when the opportunity came, Linda didn't see the need, since Willy was already on such a great career path.
    c. They had a disagreement about the terms of the offer. Willy wanted to be partners, but Ben didn't. Neither would compromise so they cancelled the deal.
    d. Linda refused to leave her friends and familiar surroundings.

7. Ben says. "What are you building? Lay your hands on it. Where is it?" What is the point of this line?
    a. Every man must take care of himself.
    b. Ben thinks Willy would have been better off as a construction worker.
    c. In fact, Willy hasn't done much worthwhile with his life. He is in debt, he is a failure at business, and his boys appear to be just like him.
    d. Ben is trying to provoke Willy just enough to motivate him, but it doesn't work.

8. Where does Willy go after his conversation with Howard?
    a. He goes to church and goes to confession.
    b. He goes to his doctor to get a prescription for sleeping pills.
    c. He goes to buy a new car.
    d. He goes to see Charley for money to cover his life insurance premium payment.

9. Willy wants to find out what went wrong with Biff, why he didn't do anything with his life after the age of 17. Who does he ask?
    a. He asks Bernard.
    b. He asks Linda.
    c. He asks Charley.
    d. He asks Happy.

10. What reply does he receive?
    a. Biff has a learning disability and never received the proper help to compensate for it.
    b. He was suffering from depression.
    c. Biff was ready to got to summer school to make up the math class, but when he returned from Boston, he gave up.
    d. There is really nothing wrong; Biff is just lazy and stubborn.

Multiple Choice Study Guide Questions - *Death of a Salesman* - Page Nine

11. Why can't Willy work for Charley?
    a. Charley stands for the things Willy does not believe in; if Willy would work for Charley, he would admit that his whole life had been wrong.
    b. Charley's business is not doing well. He doesn't have enough money to hire anyone else.
    c. Charley doesn't think Willy will do a good job, but he doesn't want to spoil their friendship by saying so.
    d. Willy's mind has been affected and he is really not capable of working a full-time job.

12. Biff says, ". . . I realized what a ridiculous lie my whole life has been." What does he mean?
    a. He finally learns that he was adopted, and he is angry that his parents never told him.
    b. He realized that he was raised on a false philosophy, and that most of the things that happened were glossed over and made far better than they were. Bill realized that he was a Clerk and a thief.
    c. He realized that he has wasted his life because he never admitted that he was afraid to be successful.
    d. He realized that he really did love his father, and it was time to admit it.

13. What was the result of Biff's meeting with Bill Oliver?
    a. He got part of the money, with a promise of more if he made good.
    b. He got brushed aside. He would never get the money, and he would have no more meetings with Bill Oliver.
    c. He got all of the money and Bill's full support.
    d. Oliver gave him a year to prove his could be responsible; then he would get the money.

14. What does Happy want Biff to tell Willy?
    a. He wants Biff to paint a glossy picture of the meeting with Oliver instead of telling the truth.
    b. He wants Biff to tell Willy he will stay home and get a job.
    c. He wants Biff to tell Willy the truth about what happened with Bill Oliver so many years ago.
    d. He wants Biff to make Willy realize his (Willy's) days as a salesman are over.

Multiple Choice Study Guide Questions - *Death of a Salesman* - Page Ten

15. Willy says, ". . . the woods are burning, boys. Can't you understand? There's a big blaze going on all around." What does that mean?
    a. Willy is having a flashback to a time in his youth when he set the woods in back of his house on fire.
    b. Times are changing. He thinks he is on the brink of a wave of good fortune.
    c. Willy's world is falling apart. He had lost his job and has no resources. He is getting trapped by the years of lies he has lived.
    d. Willy thinks he is dying, and he is contemplating the afterlife. He is afraid he will be punished for his life.

16. What does Willy do while Biff is trying to explain the facts of his meeting with Bill Oliver?
    a. He shouts curses to drown out Biff's voice.
    b. He daydreams of the time Biff flunked math.
    c. He washes and waxes the car.
    d. He takes notes so he can refer to them later.

17. What did Biff take from Bill Oliver?
    a. He took a silver picture frame.
    b. He took a fountain pen.
    c. He took a twenty dollar bill.
    d. He took the keys to the office.

18. Identify Miss Forsythe and Letta.
    a. They are women who come into the restaurant. Happy is more interested in getting a date with them than in the welfare of his own father.
    b. Miss Forsythe was Willy's high school English teacher, who had great faith in him. Letta was her daughter. She had a crush on Willy
    c. They are women who work in the office of the company Willy works for. Miss Forsythe ridicules him, but Letta feels sorry for him.
    d. They are friends and confidants of Linda's. They have offered to help her if anything ever happens to Willy.

19. Where does Willy go?
    a. He goes to the river to look at the water.
    b. He goes to the parking lot for a cigarette.
    c. He goes to the restroom to compose himself.
    d. He goes home to cry and get drunk.

Multiple Choice Study Guide Questions - *Death of a Salesman* - Page Eleven

20. What is Biff's opinion of his father now, when he tells it to Miss Forsythe?
    a. Biff says he is a "poor, wretched loser."
    b. Biff says he is a "fine, troubled prince."
    c. Biff says he is a "gentle daydreamer."
    d. Biff says he is a "nasty, selfish braggart."

21. Why can't Biff help Willy?
    a. He promised his mother he would not help.
    b. He just doesn't want to.
    c. He is afraid Happy will get jealous.
    d. They both get frustrated and yell at each other.

22. Happy denies that Willy is his father. Why?
    a. Happy doesn't want the responsibility of caring for Willy.
    b. He had secretly found proof of his adoption, and now wants the truth to be known.
    c. Happy is angry because Willy is leaving all of his money (in his will) to Biff.
    d. He does not want to admit that he is a lot like his father.

23. What happened in Boston? What do we finally find out is the problem, the secret between Willy and Biff?
    a. Biff discovered that Willy had embezzled some money. He lost his respect for Willy.
    b. They went out drinking together. On the way home, Willy ran over a man and didn't stop to help him. Biff never forgave him.
    c. Biff went to talk to his father and walked in on Willy and the woman with whom he was having an affair.
    d. Biff discovered that Willy is an alcoholic. Willy denied it, and refused to get help.

24. Why did Biff go to Boston in the first place?
    a. He went to borrow some money.
    b. He went because he wanted to get his father's signature so he could join the marines.
    c. He wanted to convince his father to let him go on the road, too. This was their first trial trip together.
    d. He went to ask Willy to talk his teacher into changing a grade so he wouldn't have to go to summer school.

Multiple Choice Study Guide Questions - *Death of a Salesman* - Page Twelve

25. Where does Willy go after he realizes that the boys have left him at the restaurant?
    a. He goes to the park for a walk.
    b. He buys some carrot seeds for his garden and goes home to plant them.
    c. He goes to buy another life insurance policy.
    d. He goes to his office to cry.

26. Why does Linda knock the flowers to the floor?
    a. She is allergic to them. She is angry because the boys knew that and brought them home anyway.
    b. It was an accident. She didn't look where she was going.
    c. She is furious because the boys left Willy at the restaurant.
    d. She is having a seizure. She was trying to keep her illness a secret from the others, so they wouldn't get upset, but she couldn't control the seizure.

27. "Willy says, " A man can't go out the way he came in, Ben, a man has got to add up to something." What does he mean.
    a. People have to take chances in life.
    b. It is better to try a lot of different jobs than to stick to one for a lifetime; he is getting ready to switch careers.
    c. He is pleasant because he raised a family.
    d. He feels like he should have contributed something to the world, and he didn't.

28. Why does Willy decide to kill himself?
    a. He can leave a lot of insurance money to Biff if his death looks like an accident. Then Biff will have a chance to be successful.
    b. He would rather die than face Linda about his past indiscretions.
    c. He is drunk and doesn't realize what he is doing.
    d. He knew he had incurable cancer and didn't want to spend the rest of his life in pain.

29. What does Biff want to tell Willy before he is ready to go?
    a. He wants to tell Willy he was really a good father.
    b. He wants to tell Willy he has decided to join the Army.
    c. He wants to tell Willy that he (Biff) is nothing, that he accepts that now, and that he has no hard feelings towards Willy.
    d. He wants to tell Willy that he and Happy have decided to go into business together so they can take care of Willy and Linda in their retirement years.

Multiple Choice Study Guide Questions - *Death of a Salesman* - Page Thirteen

30. Biff says, "Will you take that phony dream and burn it before something happens?" What is the significance of this line?
    a. It shows that Biff is losing his temper; he is about to explode.
    b. It foreshadows Willy's death.
    c. It separates the dream/illusion motif from the "woods are burning" motif.
    d. It is the final rift in the relationship between Biff and Happy.

31. What is Willy's response to Biff's whole scene when Biff ends up crying?
    a. He tells Biff to dry up and act like a man.
    b. He hugs Linda and asks her where they have gone wrong.
    c. He thinks it is remarkable that Biff actually likes him.
    d. He feels sorry for Biff, and asks Happy to talk to him.

32. Ben says, "The jungle is dark but full of diamonds, Willy." Explain.
    a. Treasures are hidden. One must work to find them.
    b. The jungle represents death; the diamonds are the insurance money.
    c. Willy did not have the courage Ben had, which is why he failed.
    d. The sales world is a jungle, but there are some good companies. Unfortunately, Willy worked for a poor company.

33. What does Willy do?
    a. He speeds away in his car and has a fatal car accident.
    b. He trades the old car in for a new one.
    c. He speeds away and keeps going. He is never heard from again.
    d. He sells the car and gives the money to the boys.

34. Why is the car an appropriate device?
    a. It is a symbol of family togetherness.
    b. It is a symbol of Willy's search for meaning.
    c. It is a symbol of the boys' ideas about freedom.
    d. It is a symbol of Willy's philosophy for success in life in general.

35. Biff realizes that Willy's philosophy was wrong, and most of Willy's life was made up of illusion. What does he say?
    a. "He took a wrong turn miles back and never figured it out."
    b. "He was a liar and a cheat. He tried to buy our love and he failed."
    c. "He had all the wrong dreams. All, all wrong."
    d. "His brother made millions, but he only made mistakes."

Multiple Choice Study Guide Questions - *Death of a Salesman* - Page Fourteen

36. Based on the events of the play and our knowledge of the characters, what will probably happen to Biff?
    a. He will become a productive citizen in the real world.
    b. He will become an alcoholic and drink himself to death.
    c. He will steal money from Oliver and end up in jail.
    d. He will follow in his father's footsteps.

37. What will probably happen to Happy?
    a. He will support Biff and Linda.
    b. He will run off and join the Army.
    c. He will become more and more like Willy.
    d. He will take over Ben's business.

38. Linda says, "We're free and clear." Which of these is not an interpretation of her statement?
    a. Biff is free of Willy's influence.
    b. They all have free wills.
    c. They are financially free because the mortgage on the house has been paid.
    d. Willy is now free of worldly concerns.

ANSWER KEY - MULTIPLE CHOICE STUDY/QUIZ QUESTIONS
Death of a Salesman

	ACT I	ACT II
1.	A	B
2.	C	D
3.	B	A
4.	D	C
5.	D	D
6.	B	B
7.	A	C
8.	D	D
9.	C	A
10.	A	C
11.	B	A
12.	D	B
13.	B	B
14.	C	A
15.	A	C
16.	D	B
17.	B	B
18.	A	A
19.	B	C
20.	C	B
21.	A	D
22.	B	A
23.	A	C
24.	A	D
25.	B	B
26.	C	C
27.	A	D
28.	C	A
29.	D	C
30.	A	B
31.	C	C
32.		B
33.		A
34.		D
35.		C
36.		A
37.		C
38.		B

PREREADING VOCABULARY WORKSHEETS

VOCABULARY - *Death of a Salesman*

Part I: Using Prior Knowledge and Contextual Clues

Below are the sentences in which the vocabulary words appear in the text. Read the sentence. Use any clues you can find in the sentence combined with your prior knowledge, and write what you think the underlined words mean in the space provided.

1. . . . she admires him, as though his <u>mercurial</u> nature, his temper, his massive dreams and little cruelties, served her only as sharp reminders of the turbulent longings within him . . . .

2. HAPPY: *with deep <u>sentiment</u>*: Funny, Biff, y'know? Us sleeping here again? The old beds. *He pats the bed affectionately.* All the talk that went across those two beds, huh? Our whole lives.

3. HAPPY: Well, you really enjoy it on a farm? Are you content out there?   BIFF, *with rising <u>agitation</u>*:

4. You're a poet, you know that, Biff? You're an <u>idealist</u>.

5. BIFF, *with enthusiasm*: Listen, why don't you come out West with me? ...
   HAPPY, *<u>avidly</u>*: The Loman Brothers, heh?

6. HAPPY, *<u>enthralled</u>*: That's what I dream about, Biff.

7. . . . the entire house and surroundings become covered with leaves. Music <u>insinuates</u> *itself as the leaves appear.*

8. WILLY, *stopping the <u>incipient</u> argument, to Happy*: Sure, he's gotta practice with a regulation ball, doesn't he?

41

Salesman Vocabulary Worksheet Assignment 1 Continued

Part II: Determining the Meaning   Match the vocabulary words to their dictionary definitions. If there are words for which you cannot figure out the definition by contextual clues and by process of elimination, look them up in a dictionary.

___ 1. mercurial   A. enthusiastically; with great interest
___ 2. sentiment   B. beginning to exist
___ 3. agitation   C. quick and changeable in temperament
___ 4. idealist   D. disturbance; annoyance
___ 5. avidly   E. held spellbound; captivated
___ 6. enthralled   F. tender, romantic or nostalgic feeling
___ 7. insinuates   G. one who sees the best in things; a dreamer; unrealistic
___ 8. incipient   H. becomes introduced gradually

Vocabulary - *Death of a Salesman* - Reading Assignment No. 2

Part I: Using Prior Knowledge and Contextual Clues
    Below are the sentences in which the vocabulary words appear in the text. Read the sentence. Use any clues you can find in the sentence combined with your prior knowledge, and write what you think the underlined words mean in the space provided.

1. . . . I can't on a Regents! That's a state exam! They're <u>liable</u> to arrest me!

2. That man was a genius, that man was success <u>incarnate</u>!

3. He is a large man, slow of speech, <u>laconic</u>, immovable.

4. In all he says, despite what he says, there is pity, and, now, <u>trepidation</u>.

5. WILLY, as though to <u>dispel</u> his confusion he angrily stops Charley's hand

6. Is this his reward--to turn around at the age of sixty-three and find his sons, who he loved better than his life, one a <u>philandering</u> bum--

7. I've been <u>remiss</u>. I know that, Mom. But now I'll stay, and I swear to you, I'll apply myself.

8. LINDA, her voice <u>subdued</u>: What'd you have to start that for?

Salesman Vocabulary Worksheet Assignment 2 Continued

Part II: Determining the Meaning   Match the vocabulary words to their dictionary definitions. If there are words for which you cannot figure out the definition by contextual clues and by process of elimination, look them up in a dictionary.

___ 9. liable
___ 10. incarnate
___ 11. laconic
___ 12. trepidation
___ 13. dispel
___ 14. philandering
___ 15. remiss
___ 16. subdued

A. to rid one's mind of
B. made less intense; toned down; softer
C. not attending to duty; negligent; careless
D. likely; at risk of experiencing something unpleasant
E. engaging in many casual love affairs
F. personified; given a human form to
G. a state of alarm or dread
H. using few words

Vocabulary - *Death of a Salesman* - Reading Assignment No. 3

Part I: Using Prior Knowledge and Contextual Clues

Below are the sentences in which the vocabulary words appear in the text. Read the sentence. Use any clues you can find in the sentence combined with your prior knowledge, and write what you think the underlined words mean in the space provided.

1. He's heading for a change. There's no question there simply are certain men that take longer to get--<u>solidified</u>.

2. Howard is <u>intent</u> on threading the machine and only glances over his shoulder as Willy appears.

3. I bought it for <u>dictation</u>, but you can do anything with it.

4. If I had a spot I'd slam you right in, but I just don't have a single <u>solitary</u> spot.

5. There was respect, and <u>comradeship</u>, and gratitude in it.

6. WILLY, furiously: Casino! <u>Incredulously</u>: Don't you realize what today is?

7. Well, Bill Oliver . . . wants Biff very badly. Called him in from the West. Long distance, <u>carte blanche</u>, special deliveries.

8. Willy, do you want to talk <u>candidly</u>?

Salesman Vocabulary Worksheet Assignment 3 Continued

Part II: Determining the Meaning   Match the vocabulary words to their dictionary definitions. If there are words for which you cannot figure out the definition by contextual clues and by process of elimination, look them up in a dictionary.

___ 17. solidified   A. concentrating; engrossed
___ 18. intent   B. unbelievingly
___ 19. dictation   C. characterized by openness; frankly
___ 20. solitary   D. made strong, sturdy or stable
___ 21. comradeship   E. existing alone
___ 22. incredulously   F. with full permission; unrestricted authority
___ 23. carte blanche   G. to say aloud to be recorded & then written by another from the recording
___ 24. candidly   H. friendship; a friendly spirit of working together for a common purpose

Vocabulary - *Death of a Salesman* - Reading Assignment No. 4

Part I: Using Prior Knowledge and Contextual Clues

Below are the sentences in which the vocabulary words appear in the text. Read the sentence. Use any clues you can find in the sentence combined with your prior knowledge, and write what you think the underlined words mean in the space provided.

1. Suddenly raucous music is heard, and a red glow rises behind the screen at right.

2. BIFF, *agonized*: I don't know, I just--wanted to take something, I don't know. You gotta help me, Hap, I'm gonna tell Pop.

3. The gist of it is that I haven't got a story left in my head.

4. Listen, kid, I took those balls years ago, now I walk in with his fountain pen? That clinches it, don't you see? I can't face him like that! I'll try elsewhere.

5. WILLY, strikes Biff and falters away from the table: You rotten little louse! Are you spiting me?

6. The Woman's call pulls Willy back. He starts right, befuddled.

7. He's just a little overstrung, he'll be all right!

Salesman Vocabulary Worksheet Assignment 4 Continued

Part II: Determining the Meaning   Match the vocabulary words to their dictionary definitions. If there are words for which you cannot figure out the definition by contextual clues and by process of elimination, look them up in a dictionary.

___ 25. raucous
___ 26. agonized
___ 27. gist
___ 28. clinches
___ 29. falters
___ 30. befuddled
___ 31. overstrung

A. stumbles; moves unsteadily
B. main idea
C. pushed to one's emotional limits
D. suffering great anguish; struggling
E. confused
F. rough-sounding; harsh; boisterous
G. settles something conclusively

Vocabulary - *Death of a Salesman* - Reading Assignment No. 5

Part I: Using Prior Knowledge and Contextual Clues

Below are the sentences in which the vocabulary words appear in the text. Read the sentence. Use any clues you can find in the sentence combined with your prior knowledge, and write what you think the underlined words mean in the space provided.

1. Raw, <u>sensuous</u> music accompanies their speech.

2. See, the reason he hates me, Pop--one day he was late for class so I got up at the blackboard and <u>imitated</u> him. I crossed my eyes and talked with a lithp.

3. Get out of here! Go back, go back . . . Suddenly <u>striving</u> for the ordinary: This is Miss Francis, Biff, she's a buyer. They're painting her room. Go back, Miss Francis, go back . . .

4. Now look, Biff, when you grow up you'll understand about these things. You musn't--you musn't <u>overemphasize</u> a thing like this.

5. WILLY, <u>anxiously</u>: Oh, I'd better hurry.

6. She rises <u>ominously</u> and quietly and moves toward Happy, who backs up into the kitchen, afraid.

7. Hey, what're you doing up? Linda says nothing but moves toward him <u>implacably</u>. Where's Pop? He keeps backing to the right, and now Linda is in full view in the doorway . . . .

8. What am I doing in an office, making a <u>contemptuous</u>, begging fool of myself, when all I want is out there, waiting for me the minute I say I know who I am!

Salesman Vocabulary Worksheet Assignment 5 Continued

Part II: Determining the Meaning   Match the vocabulary words to their dictionary definitions. If there are words for which you cannot figure out the definition by contextual clues and by process of elimination, look them up in a dictionary.

___ 32. sensuous
___ 33. imitated
___ 34. striving
___ 35. overemphasize
___ 36. anxiously
___ 37. ominously
___ 38. implacably
___ 39. contemptuous

A. threateningly
B. place too much importance on
C. with a worried eagerness
D. appealing to the senses
E. dishonorable; disgraceful
F. copied mannerisms, actions or speech
G. struggling; working
H. in a manner showing unwillingness to make peace

ANSWER KEY - VOCABULARY
Death of a Salesman

Reading Assignment No. 1		Reading Assignment No. 2		Reading Assignment No. 3	
1.	C	9.	D	17.	D
2.	F	10.	F	18.	A
3.	D	11.	H	19.	G
4.	G	12.	G	20.	E
5.	A	13.	A	21.	H
6.	E	14.	E	22.	B
7.	H	15.	C	23.	F
8.	B	16.	B	24.	C

Reading Assignment No. 4		Reading Assignment No. 5	
25.	F	32.	D
26.	D	33.	F
27.	B	34.	G
28.	G	35.	B
29.	A	36.	C
30.	E	37.	A
31.	C	38.	H
		39.	E

DAILY LESSONS

LESSON ONE

Objectives
    1. To introduce the *Death of a Salesman* unit.
    2. To distribute books and other related materials
    3. To preview the study questions for chapters 1-3
    4. To familiarize students with the vocabulary for chapters 1-3

NOTE: In this unit (Lesson Two) you are scheduled to have a guest speaker. Make sure you have looked at Lesson Two and have made the appropriate arrangements.

    Prior to Lesson One, you need to have put up background paper on the bulletin board and to have assigned students each to bring in some sort of advertisements--from a magazine or the mail--anything that can be posted on your bulletin board.

    Also, have the part assignments worked out so you can tell students which lines they will be responsible for reading. A part assignment sheet is included for your convenience. If you prefer, you can just assign the parts on the day that they will be read to whatever students happen to be present in your class that day.

Activity #1
    Have students show their ads (tell what they are in case everyone can't see them) and let the students post them on the bulletin board in a random fashion. Take a few minutes to look at each ad, discussing what each one is trying to persuade the reader to do.

TRANSITION: In our mail, in magazines, on television, on the radio, on billboards, even on the clothes we wear, we are constantly bombarded with advertising. Someone is always trying to persuade us to buy or to do something. That's sales. He who convinces the most people to buy wins (stays in business). The play we are about to read is about a salesman who upon coming to the end of his career looks back at the reality of his life.

Activity #2
    Distribute the materials students will use in this unit. Explain in detail how students are to use these materials.

    Study Guides Students should read the study guide questions for each reading assignment prior to beginning the reading assignment to get a feeling for what events and ideas are important in the section they are about to read. After reading the section, students will (as a class or individually) answer the questions to review the important events and ideas from that section of the book. Students should keep the study guides as study materials for the unit test.

<u>Vocabulary</u>   Prior to reading a reading assignment, students will do vocabulary work related to the section of the book they are about to read. Following the completion of the reading of the book, there will be a vocabulary review of all the words used in the vocabulary assignments. Students should keep their vocabulary work as study materials for the unit test.

<u>Reading Assignment Sheet</u>   You need to fill in the reading assignment sheet to let students know by when their reading has to be completed. You can either write the assignment sheet up on a side blackboard or bulletin board and leave it there for students to see each day, or you can "ditto" copies for each student to have. In either case, you should advise students to become very familiar with the reading assignments so they know what is expected of them.

<u>Extra Activities Center</u>   The Extra Activities Packet portion of this unit contains suggestions for an extra library of related books and articles in your classroom as well as crossword and word search puzzles. Make an extra activities center in your room where you will keep these materials for students to use. (Bring the books and articles in from the library and keep several copies of the puzzles on hand.) Explain to students that these materials are available for students to use when they finish reading assignments or other class work early.

<u>Nonfiction Assignment Sheet</u>   Explain to students that they each are to read at least one non-fiction piece from the in-class library at some time during the unit. Students will fill out a nonfiction assignment sheet after completing the reading to help you evaluate their reading experiences and to help the students think about and evaluate their own reading experiences.

<u>Books</u>   Each school has its own rules and regulations regarding student use of school books. Advise students of the procedures that are normal for your school.

<u>Activity #3</u>

Explain to students that since *Death of a Salesman* is a play, you will read the play orally in class. Each person will have a specific part to read and will be graded on the way it is read. Make the part assignments so students can be practicing their parts at home so they will be able to do well on the oral reading evaluation.

NONFICTION ASSIGNMENT SHEET
(To be completed after reading the required nonfiction article)

Name _____ Date _____

Title of Nonfiction Read _____

Written By _____ Publication Date _____

I. Factual Summary: Write a short summary of the piece you read.

II. Vocabulary
    1. With which vocabulary words in the piece did you encounter some degree of difficulty?

    2. How did you resolve your lack of understanding with these words?

III. Interpretation: What was the main point the author wanted you to get from reading his work?

IV. Criticism
    1. With which points of the piece did you agree or find easy to accept? Why?

    2. With which points of the piece did you disagree or find difficult to believe? Why?

V. Personal Response: What do you think about this piece? OR How does this piece influence your ideas?

PART ASSIGNMENT SHEET - *Death of a Salesman*

Reading Assignment 1
Narrator
Linda
Willy
Happy
Biff
Bernard

Reading Assignment 2
Narrator
The Woman
Willy
Linda
Bernard
Happy
Charley
Ben
Biff

Reading Assignment 3
Narrator
Linda
Howard
Howard's son
Ben
Bernard
Happy
Biff

Salesman Part Assignment Sheet Page 2

Reading Assignment 4
Narrator
Charley
Bernard
Willy
Stanley
Happy
Girl/Miss Forsythe
Biff
Young Bernard
Operator/Page
The Woman
Letta

Reading Assignment 5
Narrator
Willy
Woman
Biff
Stanley
Happy
Linda
Ben

LESSON TWO

Objectives:
1. To show students some ways that they (and we all) are manipulated by salespeople
2. To give students the background they need to work on the project assignment

Activity

During this class period, students will listen and talk with a professional sales person who will give students some of the basic rules successful salespeople follow. One of the best sources for a speaker will be Realtors. Go to your best local real estate broker and ask him or her to come speak with your class about sales and sales techniques--how to get someone to buy something.

Be sure to leave time for students to ask questions of their own.

LESSON THREE

Objectives:
1. To make the project assignment
2. To give students time to begin working on the project

Activity

Distribute the Project Assignment Sheet. Discuss the directions in detail, and give students the remainder of this class period to begin working on the assignment.

LESSON FOUR

Objectives:
1. To help students organize their projects
2. To give students the opportunity to practice writing to inform
3. To give the teacher the opportunity to evaluate students' writing skills
4. To show students how to write a brief business plan

Activity

Distribute Writing Assignment #1. Discuss the directions in detail and give students this class period to begin working on the assignment.

LESSON FIVE

Objectives:
1. To make students think about and plan their sales presentations
2. To give students the opportunity to practice writing to persuade
3. To give the teacher the opportunity to evaluate students' writing skills

Activity

Distribute Writing Assignment #2. Discuss the directions in detail and give students the remainder of this period to work on the assignment.

PROJECT ASSIGNMENT SHEET - *Death of a Salesman*

PROMPT

You're going to walk a few miles in Willy's shoes. Your class is going to have a fund raising project, and all of you are going to be salespeople for a couple of weeks.

THE GOAL

First, we have to decide for what purpose we are going to raise funds. Some suggestions are: money for more books and supplies for your English Department or Media Center, money for a field trip to see a play; money to purchase an item you want or need for your school (new stage curtains, sports or band equipment, better lights, a security system, etc.), money to bring an event or special person to your school, or money which could be donated to the charity or cause of your choice (for the homeless in your area, for MADD, for the "Just Say No!" campaign, for the March of Dimes, for The United Way, etc.).

THE PRODUCT

What will we sell? The answer to that one is easy: the thing you can get for the least amount of money and sell for the most amount of money to the most people.

If you are raising money for new books for your English Department or Media center, you might consider having a campaign to collect good, used books (which would be donated) and then sell them each for .25 to $1.00 (depending on the condition of the book).

Take a few minutes to brainstorm ideas together as a class.

THE REQUIREMENTS

This is a group project only in that you are all working for the same common cause: to raise money for your common goal. Each one of you will be responsible for:
 1. Making a sales plan
 2. Working out a sales pitch
 3. Actually selling the product
 4. Evaluating your performance and the performance of the class

THE REWARDS

If you are raising money for some *thing* for the school, you will have the reward of seeing that thing purchased (assuming it is an approved item!).

If you are donating your money to a cause, you will have the satisfaction of knowing you actually did something good to help someone else.

Not enough? Negotiate with your teacher to see if any other rewards are possible. (Sell your idea for a reward to your teacher! Use the art of persuasion!)

WRITING ASSIGNMENT #1 - *Death of a Salesman*

PROMPT
You should know now what you are going to sell and why you are going to sell it. The question that is left is, "How?". That's what you have to decide next. Your assignment is to make a sales plan; a plan that gives step-by-step details about how you plan to achieve your goal.

PREWRITING
Answer these questions:
1. How much money do you want to make?
2. How many widgets (a common name for whatever is being sold) do you need to sell to earn that much money?
3. How many people will you need to contact to sell that many widgets?
4. Who will you contact?
5. How will you contact them?
6. When will you contact them?
7. What if you haven't made enough sales by the time this supply of contacts runs out? Where will you go next?

DRAFTING
Use the usual heading you put on all your papers, with your name, class, date, etc. Title your paper, "Sales Plan."

Begin with the heading, "Goal." In this section describe what your goal is; how much money you want to make and how many widgets you have to sell to make that much money.

Your next heading is, "Contacts." In this section, write down exactly who you will contact. You may use groups of people instead of individual names, if you like.

Your next heading is, "Scheduling." In this section give the schedule of when and where you will contact the people listed under "Contacts."

Your next heading is, "Plan B." In this section, explain what you will do if you haven't reached your goal by the time you have run out of people in your "Contact" section.

Your final heading is, "Summary." In this section, summarize your plan.

PROMPT
When you finish the rough draft of your paper, ask a student who sits near you to read it. After reading your rough draft, he/she should tell you what he/she liked best about your work, which parts were difficult to understand, and ways in which your work could be improved. Reread your paper considering your critic's comments, and make the corrections you think are necessary.

PROOFREADING
Do a final proofreading of your paper double-checking your grammar, spelling, organization, and the clarity of your ideas.

WRITING ASSIGNMENT #2 - *Death of a Salesman*

PROMPT
You know what you are selling, why you are selling it, who you're going to contact and when you are going to contact them. What are you going to say when you see your contacts? After all, that's where the sale is made or lost. Your assignment is to write yourself a script to memorize; make a persuasive sales script.

PREWRITING
First, make a list of all the reasons why someone should buy your widget.
Next make a list of all the reasons why someone would not buy your widget.
Finally, make a list of things to say to overcome the client's objections (overcome reasons why he/she wouldn't buy your widget).

DRAFTING
Write a sentence of introduction in which you introduce yourself and your cause.
Explain what your widget is, what the cost is, and what the client gets for his/her money.
State what you think is (or has proven to be) the most common objection, and give your counter to it.
Give your two best reasons why a person should buy your widget.
Ask the client to purchase your widget, and stop.

When you are actually on a sales call, you should stop here and give the client a few minutes to digest your information. One of three things will happen. The client will say, "Yes," or, "No," or the client will ask questions. If the client says, "Yes," proceed with your sale. If the client has questions, answer them to the best of your ability. If you cannot answer the question, tell your client you will find the answer and report back to him/her. (And then be sure you do it!) If the client says, "No," try to find out *why* the answer is, "No." Perhaps it is a reason you have thought of (in your prewriting above) and have already found a way to overcome. If so, try to overcome the objection.

EXAMPLE: "Hello, my name is _____. My English class at school is trying to raise money to buy more books for our media center by selling widgets. These widgets are handy items that you can use for _____. They're made of sturdy, yet lightweight plastic and come in a variety of colors. If you don't want one for yourself, perhaps you would buy one as a gift for a friend. These widgets make opening cans much easier, and they also have a corkscrew on the other end. You really get two tools in one! Would you buy a widget to help us out?

PROMPT
When you finish the rough draft of your paper, ask a student who sits near you to read it. After reading your rough draft, he/she should tell you what he/she liked best about your work, which parts were difficult to understand, and ways in which your work could be improved. Reread your paper considering your critic's comments, and make the corrections you think are necessary.

PROOFREADING
Do a final proofreading of your paper double-checking your grammar, spelling, organization, and the clarity of your ideas.

LESSON SIX

Objectives
1. To preview the study questions for Act One
2. To do the prereading vocabulary work for Reading Assignment 1
3. To read Reading Assignment 1
4. To give students practice reading orally
5. To evaluate students' oral reading

Activity #1
Give students about fifteen minutes to look over the study questions for Act One and to do the prereading vocabulary work for Reading Assignment 1.

Activity #2
Have students read the parts they have been assigned. If you have not yet completed an oral reading evaluation for your students this marking period, this would be a good opportunity to do so. A form is included with this unit for your convenience.

Students should also complete the prereading vocabulary work for Reading Assignment 2 prior to your next class period.

ORAL READING EVALUATION - *Death of a Salesman*

Name _____ Class____ Date _____

SKILL	EXCELLENT	GOOD	AVERAGE	FAIR	POOR
Fluency	5	4	3	2	1
Clarity	5	4	3	2	1
Audibility	5	4	3	2	1
Pronunciation	5	4	3	2	1
_____	5	4	3	2	1
_____	5	4	3	2	1

Total _____ Grade _____

Comments:

LESSON SEVEN

Objectives:
1. To read Reading Assignment 2
2. To preview the study questions for Act Two
3. To do the prereading vocabulary work for Reading Assignment 3

Activity #1
   Read Reading Assignment 2 by having students continue to read their assigned parts orally. Continue the oral reading evaluations.

Activity #2
   Tell students that prior to your next class period they should preview the study questions for Act Two and do the prereading vocabulary work for Reading Assignment 3

LESSON EIGHT

Objectives:
1. To review the main events and ideas from Act One
2. To read Reading Assignment 3
3. To continue the oral reading evaluations

Activity #1
   Give students a few minutes to formulate answers for the study guide questions for Act One, and then discuss the answers to the questions in detail. Write the answers on the board or overhead transparency so students can have the correct answers for study purposes. Note: It is a good practice in public speaking and leadership skills for individual students to take charge of leading the discussions of the study questions. Perhaps a different student could go to the front of the class and lead the discussion each day that the study questions are discussed during this unit. Of course, the teacher should guide the discussion when appropriate and be sure to fill in any gaps the students leave.

Activity #2
   Have students continue their oral reading of *Death of a Salesman*. Today they are scheduled to be reading Reading Assignment 3.

Activity #3
   Tell students that prior to the next class period they should have completed the prereading vocabulary work for Reading Assignment 4.

LESSON NINE

Objectives:
   1. To read Reading Assignment 4
   2. To do the prereading vocabulary work for Reading Assignment 5

Activity #1
   Read Reading Assignment 4 by having students continue to read their assigned parts orally. Continue the oral reading evaluations.

Activity #2
   Tell students that prior to your next class period they should do the prereading vocabulary work for Reading Assignment 5.

LESSON TEN

Objectives
   1. To complete reading *Death of a Salesman*
   2. To complete the oral reading evaluations

Activity
   Have students complete reading *Death of a Salesman* orally. If you have not yet completed the oral reading evaluations, do so in this class period.

LESSON ELEVEN

Objectives:
    1. To review the main ideas and events from Act Two
    2. To discuss *Death of a Salesman* on interpretive and critical levels

Activity #1

    Take time at the beginning of the period to review the study questions for Act Two.

Activity #2

    Choose the questions from the Extra Discussion Questions/Writing Assignments which seem most appropriate for your students. A class discussion of these questions is most effective if students have been given the opportunity to formulate answers to the questions prior to the discussion. To this end, you may either have all the students formulate answers to all the questions, divide your class into groups and assign one or more questions to each group, or you could assign one question to each student in your class. The option you choose will make a difference in the amount of class time needed for this activity.

Activity #3

    After students have had ample time to formulate answers to the questions, begin your class discussion of the questions and the ideas presented by the questions. Be sure students take notes during the discussion so they have information to study for the unit test.

EXTRA WRITING ASSIGNMENTS/DISCUSSION QUESTIONS - *Death of a Salesman*

Interpretation

1. Where is the climax of the play? Justify your answer.

2. What are the main conflicts in the play, and how is each resolved?

3. What is the setting of the play? Why is it important? What does it add to the story?

4. Who is the central character of the play? Why?

Critical

5. Describe Willy's relationship with Biff.

6. Are Willy's actions believably motivated? Explain why or why not.

7. Describe Willy's relationship with Happy.

8. Characterize Arthur Miller's style of writing. How does it contribute to the value of the play?

9. Compare and contrast Happy and Biff.

10. Who is responsible for Willy's situation? Why?

11. Define "successful."

12. Compare and contrast Willy and Ben.

13. Explain Charley's role in the play. Why was he included?

14. How is Linda's personality important to the story?

15. Are the characters in *Death of a Salesman* stereotypes? If so, explain why Arthur Miller used stereotypes. If not, explain how the characters merit individuality.

16. What was Willy's problem?

17. Why is the episode about Willy's little affair included in the story?

18. Discuss the use of illusion in the story.

19. Discuss the importance and the roles of Ben, Howard's son, Bernard, and Linda in *Death of a Salesman*.

Death of a Salesman Extra Discussion Questions page 2

<u>Critical/Personal Response</u>
20. Could anything have been gained by including more scenes from the time before the events of the story? If so, what could have been added and for what purpose? If not, explain why not.

21. Are Happy and Biff good sons? Why or why not?

22. How would the story and its effect have changed if Willy hadn't died? Why did Arthur Miller "kill off" Willy?

23. Do you think the sibling relationship between Happy and Biff is realistic? Explain why or why not.

24. Who is responsible for Willy's death?

<u>Personal Response</u>
25. Did you enjoy reading *Death of a Salesman*? Why or why not?

26. Suppose Biff would tell about the events of this story a few years after it happened. What do you think he would say?

27. Do you know any people like any of the characters in the play? Change the real person's name so his/her identity remains anonymous and describe how he or she is like a particular character.

28. Define "success."

29. How important is being well-liked to being successful?

30. Illusion versus reality is a major theme in the play. Most people, like Willy, try to make themselves appear in the best possible way to their families and friends. Why?

31. Do you ever feel "boxed in" like Willy does? Explain.

LESSON TWELVE

Objective
> To review all of the vocabulary work done in this unit

Activity
> Choose one (or more) of the vocabulary review activities listed below and spend your class period as directed in the activity. Some of the materials for these review activities are located in the Extra Activities Packet in this unit.

VOCABULARY REVIEW ACTIVITIES

1. Divide your class into two teams and have an old-fashioned spelling or definition bee.

2. Give each of your students (or students in groups of two, three or four) a *Death of a Salesman* Vocabulary Word Search Puzzle. The person (group) to find all of the vocabulary words in the puzzle first wins.

3. Give students a *Death of a Salesman* Vocabulary Word Search Puzzle without the word list. The person or group to find the most vocabulary words in the puzzle wins.

4. Use a *Death of a Salesman* Vocabulary Crossword Puzzle. Put the puzzle onto a transparency on the overhead projector (so everyone can see it), and do the puzzle together as a class.

5. Give students a *Death of a Salesman* Vocabulary Matching Worksheet to do.

6. Divide your class into two teams. Use the *Death of a Salesman* vocabulary words with their letters jumbled as a word list. Student 1 from Team A faces off against Student 1 from Team B. You write the first jumbled word on the board. The first student (1A or 1B) to unscramble the word wins the chance for his/her team to score points. If 1A wins the jumble, go to student 2A and give him/her a definition. He/she must give you the correct spelling of the vocabulary word which fits that definition. If he/she does, Team A scores a point, and you give student 3A a definition for which you expect a correctly spelled matching vocabulary word. Continue giving Team A definitions until some team member makes an incorrect response. An incorrect response sends the game back to the jumbled-word face off, this time with students 2A and 2B. Instead of repeating giving definitions to the first few students of each team, continue with the student after the one who gave the last incorrect response on the team. For example, if Team B wins the jumbled-word face-off, and student 5B gave the last incorrect answer for Team B, you would start this round of definition questions with student 6B, and so on. The team with the most points wins!

7. Have students write a story in which they correctly use as many vocabulary words as possible. Have students read their compositions orally! Post the most original compositions on your bulletin board!

LESSONS THIRTEEN AND FOURTEEN

Objectives
1. To discuss the further development of the themes of the play
2. To give students a chance to work together in small groups to exchange ideas and find information

Activity #1
Divide your class into 4 groups - one group for each:

1. What was Willy's philosophy?
2. Put Biff's life into chronological order (given the events shown in the play) to show his growth and development as a person (character).
3. Find and explain the major symbols used in the play including (but not limited to) the flute, stockings, Ben, the woods/jungle, the football game, and the seeds/garden.
4. Define the relationships between these characters:

Willy/Linda	Willy/Ben
Willy/Charley	Happy/Biff
Biff/Willy	Happy/Willy

Allow the groups time to do their assignments. The groups should appoint a spokesperson to report the group's thoughts.

Activity #2
Use the groups' work as a nucleus and a springboard for discussions about these ideas in the play. Ask the groups' spokespersons to give the group's thoughts about their topics. Jot these down. Ask if anyone from the group has anything to add.

Take the time to discuss each idea thoroughly with the class and be sure to allow time for students (either members of the group or other class members) to express their ideas or ask questions.

Activity #3
Give students time to repair, review and study their notes from this class session and the class session from Lesson Eleven (the Extra Discussion Questions).

LESSON FIFTEEN

Objectives:
1. To give students the opportunity to complete the nonfiction reading assignment
2. To give students the opportunity to get books for personal reading for pleasure
3. To have students read nonfiction related to the story so they can relate some of the ideas in the story to the real world

Activity

Take students to the library so they can find periodical articles and other nonfiction relating to *Death of a Salesman*. Suggest that students read articles from magazines like *Nation's Business, Money, Entrepreneur,* or other business-related magazines and newspapers. Students could research career opportunities in sales, and the training necessary to be able to take advantage of these opportunities. They could read about family relationships or information about hotlines for people who are depressed or "boxed in." --Any topic relating in some way to *Death of a Salesman* is acceptable.

If some students have already completed their nonfiction reading assignments on their own time, they may get a book to read for pleasure.

LESSON SIXTEEN

Objectives:
1. To evaluate the project assignment
2. To give students the opportunity to express their personal opinions
3. To give the teacher the opportunity to evaluate student's writing

Activity #1

Take a few minutes at the beginning of the class to close your project. That is, collect final orders & final money (if applicable). Tally up and show the class how much they all made together. Determine whether or not the class made it's sales goal. In general, bring the project to a close.

Activity #2

Distribute Writing Assignment #3. Discuss the directions in detail and give students the remainder of this class time to work on this assignment.

WRITING ASSIGNMENT #3 - *Death of a Salesman*

PROMPT
Your sales project is over; you either have or have not met your goal. Now it is time to evaluate your project. Your assignment is to give your opinion about the degree of success you had with your sales project.

PREWRITING
Answer these questions:
1. Did you meet your sales goal?
2. If so, to what do you attribute your success? If not, to what do you attribute your lack of sales?
3. What things have you learned by doing this project?
4. Did this project turn out to be what you expected it to be?
5. If you were going to do this project again, what would you do differently?

DRAFTING
Write a paragraph of introduction in which you state what your goal was and whether or not you achieved it.

Write a paragraph in which you explain why you did (or did not) meet your goal.

Write a paragraph in which you tell what you would do differently if you were to do this project again.

Write a paragraph in which you explain whether or not this project was what you expected it to be.

Write a paragraph explaining what you learned by doing this project.

Write a paragraph summarizing your evaluation of your project.

PROMPT
When you finish the rough draft of your paper, ask a student who sits near you to read it. After reading your rough draft, he/she should tell you what he/she liked best about your work, which parts were difficult to understand, and ways in which your work could be improved. Reread your paper considering your critic's comments, and make the corrections you think are necessary.

PROOFREADING
Do a final proofreading of your paper double-checking your grammar, spelling, organization, and the clarity of your ideas.

LESSON SEVENTEEN

Objectives
1. To widen the breadth of students' knowledge about the topics discussed or touched upon in *Death of a Salesman*
2. To check students' nonfiction reading assignments

Activity

Ask each student to give a brief oral report about the nonfiction work he/she read for the nonfiction reading assignment. Your criteria for evaluating this report will vary depending on the level of your students. You may wish for students to give a complete report without using notes of any kind, or you may want students to read directly from a written report, or you may want to do something in between these two extremes. Just make students aware of your criteria in ample time for them to prepare their reports.

Start with one student's report. After that, ask if anyone else in the class has read on a topic related to the first student's report. If no one has, choose another student at random. After each report, be sure to ask if anyone has a report related to the one just completed. That will help keep a continuity during the discussion of the reports.

LESSON EIGHTEEN

Objective
    To review the main ideas presented in *Death of a Salesman*

Activity #1
    Choose one of the review games/activities included in the packet and spend your class period as outlined there. Some materials for these activities are located in the Extra Activities Packet section of this unit.

Activity #2
    While students are doing the review activities, call individual students to your desk or some other private area and hold a conference in which you discuss the student's writing for this unit. An evaluation sheet is provided with this unit for your convenience to help you structure your conferences.

Activity #3
    Remind students that the Unit Test will be in the next class meeting. Stress the review of the Study Guides and their class notes as a last minute, brush-up review for homework.

WRITING EVALUATION FORM - *Death of a Salesman*

Name _____ Date _____

    Grade _____

Circle One For Each Item:

Grammar: correct   errors noted on paper

Spelling: correct   errors noted on paper

Punctuation: correct   errors noted on paper

Legibility: excellent   good   fair   poor

Strengths:

Weaknesses:

Comments/Suggestions:

REVIEW GAMES/ACTIVITIES - *Death of a Salesman*

1. Ask the class to make up a unit test for *Death of a Salesman*. The test should have 4 sections: matching, true/false, short answer, and essay. Students may use 1/2 period to make the test and then swap papers and use the other 1/2 class period to take a test a classmate has devised. (open book) You may want to use the unit test included in this packet or take questions from the students' unit tests to formulate your own test.

2. Take 1/2 period for students to make up true and false questions (including the answers). Collect the papers and divide the class into two teams. Draw a big tic-tac-toe board on the chalk board. Make one team X and one team O. Ask questions to each side, giving each student one turn. If the question is answered correctly, that students' team's letter (X or O) is placed in the box. If the answer is incorrect, no mark is placed in the box. The object is to get three marks in a row like tic-tac-toe. You may want to keep track of the number of games won for each team.

3. Take 1/2 period for students to make up questions (true/false and short answer). Collect the questions. Divide the class into two teams. You'll alternate asking questions to individual members of teams A & B (like in a spelling bee). The question keeps going from A to B until it is correctly answered, then a new question is asked. A correct answer does not allow the team to get another question. Correct answers are +2 points; incorrect answers are -1 point.

4. Have students pair up and quiz each other from their study guides and class notes.

5. Give students a *Death of a Salesman* crossword puzzle to complete.

6. Divide your class into two teams. Use the *Death of a Salesman* crossword words with their letters jumbled as a word list. Student 1 from Team A faces off against Student 1 from Team B. You write the first jumbled word on the board. The first student (1A or 1B) to unscramble the word wins the chance for his/her team to score points. If 1A wins the jumble, go to student 2A and give him/her a clue. He/she must give you the correct word which matches that clue. If he/she does, Team A scores a point, and you give student 3A a clue for which you expect another correct response. Continue giving Team A clues until some team member makes an incorrect response. An incorrect response sends the game back to the jumbled-word face off, this time with students 2A and 2B. Instead of repeating giving clues to the first few students of each team, continue with the student after the one who gave the last incorrect response on the team. For example, if Team B wins the jumbled-word face-off, and student 5B gave the last incorrect answer for Team B, you would start this round of clue questions with student 6B, and so on. The team with the most points wins!

UNIT TESTS

SHORT ANSWER UNIT TEST 1 - *Death of a Salesman*

I. Matching/Identify

____ 1. Ben   A. Happy tries to pick her up at the restaurant

____ 2. Bernard   B. Willy's wife

____ 3. Biff   C. Willy's oldest son

____ 4. Charley   D. Bill; Biff wants to borrow money from him

____ 5. Forsythe   E. Willy's brother

____ 6. Happy   F. The salesman

____ 7. Howard   G. Willy's last name

____ 8. Linda   H. Charley's son

____ 9. Loman   I. Author

____ 10. Miller   J. He fires Willy

____ 11. Oliver   K. He loans Willy money

____ 12. Willy   L. Biff's brother

Salesman Short Answer Unit Test 1 Page 2

II. Short Answer

1. Happy says, "I don't know what to do about him [Willy], it's getting embarrassing." To what is he referring and what does the fact that he says this tell us about his character?

2. Charley says, "To hell with it. When a deposit bottle is broken, you don't get your nickel back." What does he mean?

3. Linda says, "Attention, attention must be paid to such a person." Explain.

4. "You can't eat the orange and throw the peel away -- a man isn't a piece of fruit!" Explain why Willy said that.

5. "This is no time for false pride, Willy. . . . You've got two great boys, haven't you?" What is sadly ironic about this statement?

6. Why didn't Willy go with Ben years ago when Ben offered him a job?

Salesman Short Answer Unit Test 1 Page 3

7. Why can't Willy work for Charley?

8. Willy says, ". . . the woods are burning, boys, can't you understand? There's a big blaze going on all around." What does that mean?

9. What happened in Boston?

10. "The jungle is full of diamonds, Willy." Explain.

11. "He had all the wrong dreams. All, all wrong." Explain.

12. Linda says, "We're free and clear." Explain the double meaning of her words.

Salesman Short Answer Unit Test 1 Page 4

III. Composition

What is the point of *Death of a Salesman*? When we read books, we usually come away from our reading experience a little richer, having given more thought to a particular aspect of life. What do you think we're intended to gain from reading this play?

IV. Vocabulary

Listen to the vocabulary words and write them down.
Go back later and fill in the correct definition for each word.

1.

2.

3.

4.

5.

6.

7.

8.

9.

10.

SHORT ANSWER UNIT TEST 2 - *Death of a Salesman*

I. Matching/Identify

____ 1. Ben   A. Charley's son

____ 2. Bernard   B. Author

____ 3. Biff   C. He fires Willy

____ 4. Charley   D. He loans Willy money

____ 5. Forsythe   E. Bill; Biff wants to borrow money from him

____ 6. Oliver   K. Willy's brother

____ 7. Happy   F. Biff's brother

____ 8. Howard   G. Willy's last name

____ 9. Linda   H. Happy tries to pick her up at the restaurant

____ 10. Loman   I. Willy's wife

____ 11. Miller   J. Willy's oldest son

____ 12. Willy   L. The salesman

Salesman Short Answer Unit Test 2 Page 2

II. Short Answer

1. What is Linda's reaction to Willy's complaints about himself?

2. What seems to be the problem between Biff and Willy?

3. Why does Willy talk so much about the car?

4. What does Willy mean, "I'll make it up to you, Linda, I'll --"? What does Linda think he means?

5. What did Willy's father do for a living? How is that different from what Willy does?

6. Why didn't Willy go with Ben years ago when Ben offered him a job?

7. Ben says. "What are you building? Lay your hands on it. Where is it?" What is the point of this line?

Salesman Short Answer Unit Test 2 Page 3

8. Biff says, ". . . I realized what a ridiculous lie my whole life has been." What does he mean?

9. Why can't Biff help Willy?

10. Happy denies that Willy is his father. Why?

11. Willy says, "A man can't go out the way he came in, Ben, a man has got to add up to something." What does he mean?

12. Why does Willy decide to kill himself?

13. Biff says, "Will you take that phony dream and burn it before something happens?" What is the significance of this line?

14. Why is the car an appropriate device for Willy's suicide?

15. Biff says, "He had all the wrong dreams. All, all wrong." Explain.

Salesman Short Answer Unit Test 2 Page 4

III. Composition
    Is *Death of a Salesman* a tragedy? Explain why or why not.

IV. Vocabulary Write down the vocabulary words as you hear them. Go back later and write down their definitions.

   1.

   2.

   3.

   4.

   5.

   6.

   7.

   8.

   9.

   10.

KEY: SHORT ANSWER UNIT TESTS - *Death of a Salesman*

The short answer questions are taken directly from the study guides.
If you need to look up the answers, you will find them in the study guide section.

Answers to the composition questions will vary depending on your
class discussions and the level of your students.

For the vocabulary section of the test, choose ten of the
words from the vocabulary lists to read orally for your students.

The answers to the matching section of the test are below.

Answers to the matching section of the Advanced Short Answer Unit Test
are the same as for Short Answer Unit Test #2.

<u>Test #1</u>
1. E
2. H
3. C
4. K
5. A
6. L
7. J
8. B
9. G
10. I
11. D
12. F

<u>Test #2</u>
1. K
2. A
3. J
4. D
5. H
6. E
7. F
8. C
9. I
10. G
11. B
12. L

ADVANCED SHORT ANSWER UNIT TEST - *Death of a Salesman*

I. Matching/Identify

____ 1. Ben   A. Charley's son

____ 2. Bernard   B. Author

____ 3. Biff   C. He fires Willy

____ 4. Charley   D. He loans Willy money

____ 5. Forsythe   E. Bill; Biff wants to borrow money from him

____ 11. Oliver   K. Willy's brother

____ 6. Happy   F. Biff's brother

____ 7. Howard   G. Willy's last name

____ 8. Linda   H. Happy tries to pick her up at the restaurant

____ 9. Loman   I. Willy's wife

____ 10. Miller   J. Willy's oldest son

____ 12. Willy   L. The salesman

II. Short Answer
1. Compare and contrast Happy and Biff.

2. Who is responsible for Willy's situation? Why?

Salesman Advanced Short Answer Unit Test Page 2

3. Explain Charley's role in the play. Why was he included?

4. What was Willy's problem?

5. Discuss the use of illusion in the story.

6. How would the story and its effect have changed if Willy hadn't died? Why did Arthur Miller "kill off" Willy?

7. Who is responsible for Willy's death?

Salesman Advanced Short Answer Unit Test Page 3

8. Linda says, "Attention, attention must be paid to such a person." Explain.

9. Willy says, ". . . the woods are burning, boys, can't you understand? There's a big blaze going on all around." What does he mean?

10. Linda says, "We're free and clear." Explain the double meaning of her words.

Salesman Advanced Short Answer Unit Test Page 4

III. Composition

Choose three symbolic images from *Death of a Salesman* and write one paragraph about each.

Salesman Advanced Short Answer Unit Test Page 5

IV. Vocabulary

Listen to the vocabulary words and write them down. Go back later and write a composition using all of the words. The composition must relate to *Death of a Salesman*.

MULTIPLE CHOICE UNIT TEST 1 - *Death of a Salesman*

I. Matching

____ 1. Ben   A. Happy tries to pick her up at the restaurant

____ 2. Bernard   B. Willy's wife

____ 3. Biff   C. Willy's oldest son

____ 4. Charley   D. Bill; Biff wants to borrow money from him

____ 5. Forsythe   E. Willy's brother

____ 6. Happy   F. The salesman

____ 7. Howard   G. Willy's last name

____ 8. Linda   H. Charley's son

____ 9. Loman   I. Author

____ 10. Miller   J. He fires Willy

____ 11. Oliver   K. He loans Willy money

____ 12. Willy   L. Biff's brother

II. Multiple Choice

1. What is Linda's reaction to Willy's complaints about himself?
    a. She agrees and says she never should have married him.
    b. She urges him to see a therapist.
    c. She cries and says not to talk like that.
    d. She makes excuses for him.

2. What seems to be the problem between Biff and Willy?
    a. Biff is a draft dodger, and Willy wanted him to have a military career.
    b. Biff was disrespectful to his mother, and Wily was angry about it.
    c. Biff wants to move to Alaska, but Willy wants him to go into sales and take over his (Willy's) route.
    d. Biff is unsettled and hasn't made anything of himself yet, and this distress Willy.

Salesman Multiple Choice Unit Test 1 Page 2

3. What does Willy mean, "I'll make it up to you, Linda, I'll --"? What does Linda think he means?
    a. Willy means that he'll make up for his infidelity, Linda thinks he is talking about his business and will try to make more money for them.
    b. Willy means that he will pay more attention to her when he's home. She is thinking the same thing.
    c. Willy means he will make more money, Linda thinks he is talking about spending more time together.
    d. Willy means he'll spend more time with her and the boys. Linda thinks he is talking about his past indiscretions.

4. Charley says, "To hell with it. When a deposit bottle is broken, you don't get your nickel back." What does he mean?
    a. One may invest a lot of time and money into a child, but if the child doesn't turn out well, you won't get any satisfaction or rewards for your time spent. But, there's no use worrying about it; you just pick up and go on with your life.
    b. He's explaining to a client that he cannot accept returns for broken goods.
    c. If you don't live a good life, you won't have any rewards at the end of your life. In order to get to heaven, you have to be good on Earth.
    d. He is tired of listening to Willy whine about all that has gone wrong in his life, and he's just trying to cut him off short so he doesn't have to listen to him anymore.

5. How is what Willy's father did for a living different from what Willy does?
    a. Willy's father was a teacher. He traveled to teach short courses in different areas.
    b. Willy's father made flutes and sold them. Willy sells someone else's product and doesn't have the pride of craftsmanship that his father did.
    c. Willy's father was uneducated, and was never able to advance. Willy has a degree in business, although he had chosen not to make good use of it.
    d. Willy's father was an intellectual and an inventor. He had brilliant ideas but was never able to make a profit with them. Willy never though much about ideas; instead, he concentrated on making money.

Salesman Multiple Choice Unit Test 1 Page 3

6. Why does Charley tell Willy "the jails are full of fearless characters"?
    a. There has been a series of burglaries in their neighborhood. They have been discussing ways to scare away the young hoodlums.
    b. Charley's son has recently been sentenced to five years in jail for armed robbery. Charley is saving face, pretending he is not afraid for his son's safety in prison.
    c. Willy has just sent his sons across the road to a new construction site to steal more building supplies. Willy is proud of their fearlessness, but Charley sees a more practical side to it, that what the boys are doing is wrong.
    d. Willy has shared a rather shady business scheme with Charley. Charley doesn't want to participate, and Willy calls him a coward.

7. Linda says, "Attention, attention must be paid to such a person." Explain.
    a. Willy deserves our attention, our interest, and caring. Even though he is misguided, he is trying to muddle through life as well as he can.
    b. Biff is having a difficult time, and his parents should help him instead of criticizing.
    c. They would all do well to study Ben's methods for success and copy them.
    d. She thinks Charley is dangerous, and wants Willy to stop talking to him. She cites several instances that happened while Willy was away, Willy disagrees with his wife.

8. "You can't eat the orange and throw the peel away -- a man isn't a piece of fruit!" Explain why Willy said that.
    a. He is trying to convince his family he isn't crazy - "a fruitcake."
    b. He is telling his family they have to accept him the way he is, and never expect to be rich.
    c. He has spent the best years of his life working for the company, and now, in his old age, they are letting him go since there is no use for him.
    d. He finally realizes that he has to accept his own shortcomings as well as his son Biff's.

9. "This is no time for false pride, Willy. . . . You've got two great boys, haven't you?" Now that Willy really needs the boys, the reality of their worthlessness crushes his idealized version, and Willy is in a Catch-22, no win situation. Which literary element is being used here?
    a. This is a rhetorical question.
    b. This is foreshadowing.
    c. This is figurative language.
    d. This is irony.

Salesman Multiple Choice Unit Test 1 Page 4

10. Why can't Willy work for Charley?
    a. Charley stands for the things Willy does not believe in; if Willy would work for Charley, he would admit that his whole life had been wrong.
    b. Charley's business is not doing well. He doesn't have enough money to hire anyone else.
    c. Charley doesn't think Willy will do a good job, but he doesn't want to spoil their friendship by saying so.
    d. Willy's mind has been affected and he is really not capable of working a full-time job.

11. Biff says, ". . . I realized what a ridiculous lie my whole life has been." What does he mean?
    a. He finally learns that he was adopted, and he is angry that his parents never told him.
    b. He realized that he was raised on a false philosophy, and that most of the things that happened were glossed over and made far better than they were. Bill realized that he was a Clerk and a thief.
    c. He realized that he has wasted his life because he never admitted that he was afraid to be successful.
    d. He realized that he really did love his father, and it was time to admit it.

12. Willy says, ". . . the woods are burning, boys. Can't you understand? There's a big blaze going on all around." What does that mean?
    a. Willy is having a flashback to a time in his youth when he set the woods in back of his house on fire.
    b. Times are changing. He thinks he is on the brink of a wave of good fortune.
    c. Willy's world is falling apart. He had lost his job and has no resources. He is getting trapped by the years of lies he has lived.
    d. Willy thinks he is dying, and he is contemplating the afterlife. He is afraid he will be punished for his life.

13. Happy denies that Willy is his father. Why?
    a. Happy doesn't want the responsibility of caring for Willy.
    b. He had secretly found proof of his adoption, and now wants the truth to be known.
    c. Happy is angry because Willy is leaving all of his money (in his will) to Biff.
    d. He does not want to admit that he is a lot like his father.

14. Biff realizes that Willy's philosophy was wrong, and most of Willy's life was made up of illusion. What does he say?
    a. "He took a wrong turn miles back and never figured it out."
    b. "He was a liar and a cheat. He tried to buy our love and he failed."
    c. "He had all the wrong dreams. All, all wrong."
    d. "His brother made millions, but he only made mistakes."

Salesman Multiple Choice Unit Test 1 Page 5

15. Linda says, "We're free and clear." Which of these is <u>not</u> an interpretation of her statement?
    a. Biff is free of Willy's influence.
    b. They all have free wills.
    c. They are financially free because the mortgage on the house has been paid.
    d. Willy is now free of worldly concerns.

III. Composition
    Explain in detail why Willy killed himself.

Salesman Multiple Choice Unit Test 1 Page 6

IV. Vocabulary

___ 1. GIST A. Friendship; friendly spirit of working together
___ 2. OMINOUSLY B. Disturbance; annoyance
___ 3. COMRADESHIP C. Tender, romantic or nostalgic feeling
___ 4. BEFUDDLED D. Threateningly
___ 5. LIABLE E. Confused
___ 6. DISPEL F. A state of alarm or dread
___ 7. OVEREMPHASIZE G. To rid one's mind of
___ 8. REMISS H. Appealing to the senses
___ 9. TREPIDATION I. In a manner showing unwillingness to make peace
___ 10. ANXIOUSLY J. With a worried eagerness
___ 11. SENSUOUS K. Struggling; working
___ 12. OVERSTRUNG L. Main idea
___ 13. IDEALIST M. Settles something conclusively
___ 14. STRIVING N. Pushed to one's emotional limits
___ 15. AGITATION O. Likely; at risk of experiencing something unpleasant
___ 16. IMPLACABLY P. To say aloud to be recorded & then written by another from the recording
___ 17. DICTATION Q. One who sees the best in things; a dreamer; not realistic
___ 18. CLINCHES R. Place too much importance on
___ 19. SENTIMENT S. Not attending to duty; negligent; careless
___ 20. CANDIDLY T. Characterized by openness; frankly; straightforward

MULTIPLE CHOICE UNIT TEST 2 - *Death of a Salesman*

I. Matching

____ 1. Ben   A. Charley's son

____ 2. Bernard   B. Author

____ 3. Biff   C. He fires Willy

____ 4. Charley   D. He loans Willy money

____ 5. Forsythe   E. Bill; Biff wants to borrow money from him

____ 11. Oliver   K. Willy's brother

____ 6. Happy   F. Biff's brother

____ 7. Howard   G. Willy's last name

____ 8. Linda   H. Happy tries to pick her up at the restaurant

____ 9. Loman   I. Willy's wife

____ 10. Miller   J. Willy's oldest son

____ 12. Willy   L. The salesman

II. Multiple Choice
1. What is Linda's reaction to Willy's complaints about himself?
    a. She makes excuses for him..
    b. She agrees and says she never should have married him.
    c. She urges him to see a therapist.
    d. She cries and says not to talk like that.

2. What seems to be the problem between Biff and Willy?
    a. Biff is a draft dodger, and Willy wanted him to have a military career.
    b. Biff is unsettled and hasn't made anything of himself yet, and this distresses Willy.
    c. Biff wants to move to Alaska, but Willy wants him to go into sales and take over his (Willy's) route.
    d. Biff was disrespectful to his mother, and Wily was angry about it.

Salesman Multiple Choice Unit Test 2 Page 2

3. What does Willy mean, "I'll make it up to you, Linda, I'll --"? What does Linda think he means?
    a. Willy means he'll spend more time with her and the boys. Linda thinks he is talking about his past indiscretions.
    b. Willy means that he will pay more attention to her when he's home. She is thinking the same thing.
    c. Willy means he will make more money, Linda thinks he is talking about spending more time together.
    d. Willy means that he'll make up for his infidelity, Linda thinks he is talking about his business and will try to make more money for them.

4. Charley says, "To hell with it. When a deposit bottle is broken, you don't get your nickel back." What does he mean?
    a. If you don't live a good life, you won't have any rewards at the end of your life. In order to get to heaven, you have to be good on Earth.
    b. He's explaining to a client that he cannot accept returns for broken goods.
    c. One may invest a lot of time and money into a child, but if the child doesn't turn out well, you won't get any satisfaction or rewards for your time spent. But, there's no use worrying about it; you just pick up and go on with your life.
    d. He is tired of listening to Willy whine about all that has gone wrong in his life, and he's just trying to cut him off short so he doesn't have to listen to him anymore.

5. How is what Willy's father did for a living different from what Willy does?
    a. Willy's father was a teacher. He traveled to teach short courses in different areas.
    b. Willy's father was uneducated, and was never able to advance. Willy has a degree in business, although he had chosen not to make good use of it.
    c. Willy's father made flutes and sold them. Willy sells someone else's product and doesn't have the pride of craftsmanship that his father did.
    d. Willy's father was an intellectual and an inventor. He had brilliant ideas but was never able to make a profit with them. Willy never though much about ideas; instead, he concentrated on making money.

Salesman Multiple Choice Unit Test 2 Page 3

6. Why does Charley tell Willy "the jails are full of fearless characters"?
   a. Willy has just sent his sons across the road to a new construction site to steal more building supplies. Willy is proud of their fearlessness, but Charley sees a more practical side to it, that what the boys are doing is wrong.
   b. Charley's son has recently been sentenced to five years in jail for armed robbery. Charley is saving face, pretending he is not afraid for his son's safety in prison.
   c. There has been a series of burglaries in their neighborhood. They have been discussing ways to scare away the young hoodlums.
   d. Willy has shared a rather shady business scheme with Charley. Charley doesn't want to participate, and Willy calls him a coward.

7. Linda says, "Attention, attention must be paid to such a person." Explain.
   a. Biff is having a difficult time, and his parents should help him instead of criticizing.
   b. Willy deserves our attention, our interest, and caring. Even though he is misguided, he is trying to muddle through life as well as he can.
   c. They would all do well to study Ben's methods for success and copy them.
   d. She thinks Charley is dangerous, and wants Willy to stop talking to him. She cites several instances that happened while Willy was away, Willy disagrees with his wife.

8. "You can't eat the orange and throw the peel away -- a man isn't a piece of fruit!" Explain why Willy said that.
   a. He is trying to convince his family he isn't crazy - "a fruitcake."
   b. He is telling his family they have to accept him the way he is, and never expect to be rich.
   c. He finally realizes that he has to accept his own shortcomings as well as his son Biff's.
   d. He has spent the best years of his life working for the company, and now, in his old age, they are letting him go since there is no use for him.

9. "This is no time for false pride, Willy. . . . You've got two great boys, haven't you?" Now that Willy really needs the boys, the reality of their worthlessness crushes his idealized version, and Willy is in a Catch-22, no win situation. Which literary element is being used here?
   a. This is a rhetorical question.
   b. This is irony.
   c. This is figurative language.
   d. This is foreshadowing.

Salesman Multiple Choice Unit Test 2 Page 4

10. Why can't Willy work for Charley?
    a. Charley doesn't think Willy will do a good job, but he doesn't want to spoil their friendship by saying so.
    b. Charley's business is not doing well. He doesn't have enough money to hire anyone else.
    c. Charley stands for the things Willy does not believe in; if Willy would work for Charley, he would admit that his whole life had been wrong.
    d. Willy's mind has been affected and he is really not capable of working a full-time job.

11. Biff says, ". . . I realized what a ridiculous lie my whole life has been." What does he mean?
    a. He finally learns that he was adopted, and he is angry that his parents never told him.
    b. He realized that he has wasted his life because he never admitted that he was afraid to be successful.
    c. He realized that he was raised on a false philosophy, and that most of the things that happened were glossed over and made far better than they were. Bill realized that he was a Clerk and a thief.
    d. He realized that he really did love his father, and it was time to admit it.

12. Willy says, ". . . the woods are burning, boys. Can't you understand? There's a big blaze going on all around." What does that mean?
    a. Willy's world is falling apart. He had lost his job and has no resources. He is getting trapped by the years of lies he has lived.
    b. Times are changing. He thinks he is on the brink of a wave of good fortune.
    c. Willy is having a flashback to a time in his youth when he set the woods in back of his house on fire.
    d. Willy thinks he is dying, and he is contemplating the afterlife. He is afraid he will be punished for his life.

13. Happy denies that Willy is his father. Why?
    a. He does not want to admit that he is a lot like his father.
    b. He had secretly found proof of his adoption, and now wants the truth to be known.
    c. Happy is angry because Willy is leaving all of his money (in his will) to Biff.
    d. Happy doesn't want the responsibility of caring for Willy.

14. Biff realizes that Willy's philosophy was wrong, and most of Willy's life was made up of illusion. What does he say?
    a. "He took a wrong turn miles back and never figured it out."
    b. "He had all the wrong dreams. All, all wrong."
    c. "He was a liar and a cheat. He tried to buy our love and he failed."
    d. "His brother made millions, but he only made mistakes."

Salesman Multiple Choice Unit Test 2 Page 5

15. Linda says, "We're free and clear." Which of these is <u>not</u> an interpretation of her statement?
    a. Biff is free of Willy's influence.
    b. They are financially free because the mortgage on the house has been paid.
    c. They all have free wills.
    d. Willy is now free of worldly concerns.

III. Composition
    Choose one word that best describes Willy. Write a composition in which you explain why you chose that word, and in which you show off as much of your knowledge of the play as you can.

Salesman Multiple Choice Unit Test 2 Page 6

IV. Vocabulary

___ 1. COMRADESHIP   A. Enthusiastically; with great interest

___ 2. GIST   B. Held spellbound; captivated

___ 3. INSINUATES   C. Becomes introduced gradually

___ 4. SOLIDIFIED   D. Beginning to exist

___ 5. ENTHRALLED   E. Struggling; working

___ 6. REMISS   F. To rid one's mind of

___ 7. FALTERS   G. Disturbance; annoyance

___ 8. AGITATION   H. Friendship; friendly spirit of working together

___ 9. AGONIZED   I. Likely; at risk of experiencing something unpleasant

___ 10. STRIVING   J. Not attending to duty; negligent; careless

___ 11. SENSUOUS   K. Appealing to the senses

___ 12. OVERSTRUNG   L. Pushed to one's emotional limits

___ 13. AVIDLY   M. Suffering great anguish; struggling

___ 14. CONTEMPTUOUS   N. Quick & changeable in temperament

___ 15. LIABLE   O. Main idea

___ 16. DICTATION   P. Stumbles; moves unsteadily

___ 17. INCIPIENT   Q. Dishonorable; disgraceful

___ 18. DISPEL   R. Made strong, sturdy or stable

___ 19. MERCURIAL   S. To say aloud to be recorded & then written by another from the recording

___ 20. INTENT   T. Concentrating; engrossed

ANSWER SHEET - *Death of a Salesman*
Multiple Choice Unit Tests

I. Matching	II. Multiple Choice	IV. Vocabulary
1. ___	1. ___	1. ___
2. ___	2. ___	2. ___
3. ___	3. ___	3. ___
4. ___	4. ___	4. ___
5. ___	5. ___	5. ___
6. ___	6. ___	6. ___
7. ___	7. ___	7. ___
8. ___	8. ___	8. ___
9. ___	9. ___	9. ___
10. ___	10. ___	10. ___
11. ___	11. ___	11. ___
12. ___	12. ___	12. ___
	13. ___	13. ___
	14. ___	14. ___
	15. ___	15. ___
		16. ___
		17. ___
		18. ___
		19. ___
		20. ___

ANSWER KEY MULTIPLE CHOICE UNIT TESTS – *Death of a Salesman*

Answers to Unit Test 1 are in the left column. Answers to Unit Test 2 are in the right column.

I. Matching	II. Multiple Choice	IV. Vocabulary
1. E K	1. D A	1. L H
2. H A	2. D B	2. D O
3. C J	3. A D	3. A C
4. K D	4. A C	4. E R
5. A H	5. B C	5. O B
6. L E	6. C A	6. G J
7. J F	7. A B	7. R P
8. B C	8. C D	8. S G
9. G I	9. D B	9. F M
10. I G	10. A C	10. J E
11. D B	11. B C	11. H K
12. F L	12. C A	12. N L
	13. A D	13. Q A
	14. C B	14. K Q
	15. B C	15. B I
		16. I S
		17. P D
		18. M F
		19. C N
		20. T T

UNIT RESOURCE MATERIALS

BULLETIN BOARD IDEAS - *Death of a Salesman*

1. Save one corner of the board for the best of students' *Death of a Salesman* writing assignments.

2. Take one of the word search puzzles from the extra activities packet and with a marker copy it over in a large size on the bulletin board. Write the clue words to find to one side. Invite students prior to and after class to find the words and circle them on the bulletin board.

3. Write several of the most significant quotations from the book onto the board on brightly colored paper.

4. Make a bulletin board listing the vocabulary words for this unit. As you complete sections of the play and discuss the vocabulary for each section, write the definitions on the bulletin board. (If your board is one students face frequently, it will help them learn the words.)

5. Make the bulletin board as described in Lesson One.

6. Do a bulletin board about careers in sales. Your guidance office should have lots of information you can post.

7. Make a bulletin board about hotlines people who are depressed or feel "boxed in" (like Willy does) can call for help.

8. Make a bulletin board about sales techniques. Your guest speaker could probably provide materials for this one. If you're not having a guest speaker, call your local Realtor's office, or a corporation you know trains its own salespeople. Either should have plenty of information for you.

9. Post reviews of *Death of a Salesman* on your bulletin board.

10. Make a bulletin board on which you set your goal for selling your widgets (whatever it is you are going to sell as a class project), and as students turn in their sales, mark them up on the board so students can see their progress towards their goal.

EXTRA ACTIVITIES

One of the difficulties in teaching a play is that all students don't read at the same speed. One student who likes to read may take the book home and finish it in a day or two. Sometimes a few students finish the in-class assignments early. The problem, then, is finding suitable extra activities for students.

The best thing I've found is to keep a little library in the classroom. For this unit on *Death of a Salesman,* you might check out from the school library other related books and articles about careers (specifically careers in sales, management, office work, or work involving travel). You might provide information for students about financial planning and what it costs to live "on your own." A biography of the author or other works by the author would be interesting for some students.

Other things you may keep on hand are puzzles. We have made some relating directly to *Death of a Salesman* for you. Feel free to duplicate them.

Some students may like to draw. You might devise a contest or allow some extra-credit grade for students who draw characters or scenes from *Death of a Salesman.* Note, too, that if the students do not want to keep their drawings you may pick up some extra bulletin board materials this way. If you have a contest and you supply the prize (a CD or something like that perhaps), you could, possibly, make the drawing itself a non-refundable entry fee.

The pages which follow contain games, puzzles and worksheets. The keys, when appropriate, immediately follow the puzzle or worksheet. There are two main groups of activities: one group for the unit; that is, generally relating to the *Death of a Salesman* text, and another group of activities related strictly to the *Death of a Salesman* vocabulary.

Directions for these games, puzzles and worksheets are self-explanatory. The object here is to provide you with extra materials you may use in any way you choose.

MORE ACTIVITIES - *Death of a Salesman*

1. Pick a scene and have the students act it out on a stage. (Perhaps you could assign various scenes to different groups of students so more than one scene could be acted and more students could participate.)

2. Divide your class into groups of four students. Explain that they are a family of four. Each student should represent a family member--a father, a mother or a child. The group may decide the age of the children. Their family income is $25,000 per year. The group should make a list of the family's needs and wants. Then, they should make a budget to fit their needs and wants into the family income. They should make an itemized list of monthly expenses with the appropriate dollar amounts filled in. When students are finished, discuss how realistic the budgets were (or were not).

3. Use some of the related topics (noted earlier for an in-class library) as topics for research, reports or written papers, or as topics for guest speakers.

4. Have students design a playbill for *Death of a Salesman.*

5. Have students design a bulletin board (ready to be put up; not just sketched) for *Death of a Salesman.*

6. Students could research and report on reasons for suicide and/or ways to deal with stress.

7. Have someone from a family counseling center come to talk to students about family relationships or common family problems and how they can be resolved.

8. Have students pretend to be one of the characters in the play and write a letter to a friend about their family situation (prior to Willy's death). The objective here is to study point of view.

9. Make a full production of the play and perform it for your school.

10. Have students write a rap song or lyrics to a melody they already know about the life of Willy Loman. Have students perform their songs either live or on tape. If they do it on audio tape, they can remain somewhat anonymous and yet everyone can enjoy their work.

WORD SEARCH - *Death of a Salesman*

All words in this list are associated with *Death of a Salesman*. The words are placed backwards, forward, diagonally, up and down. The included words are listed below the word searches.

```
P F D J L Q Y B X B W N S N K K L P C V N H N F
W M R O Z R W J P Z C O S Z E I X T E O L C M L
R Z M E D B J D N A Q L O Y N I T Y N E A O S F
C A R D S M A E R D P R I D E O L I V E R C R S
N K N D F T P F L A D V A P S L C Q U T W F H M
W R E C K O A R L T W N R J I K R H G R T N S J
M E J X H R O U E U T O A W E L P A B H F F P J
S E S U C X E T R M T A H L B A G R H W O M A N
P R H C N X I L B A I E C S G E T N I C D I T F
K G E T Z G V N L A N U S H N N R T C N L F F L
W D Q W Y Z L H S I L T M A A Q E N E S C I Z N
B E N M S S K E G U M L M Y M P C W A N B E P S
Y Z H M T N R G V F R S B G T J P X E R T J N M
X J B X L T A O F J E A G Z L D R Y G N D I L P
H D X L V K S H F L B R N B C O M M I S S I O N
D I A M O N D S A T T Y B C L Y M N G V W R T N
X D F X D M X S Y F G H C Y E Y T W J C R Q W S
```

ANSWERS	DIAMONDS	JAILS	PREMIUM
ATTENTION	DREAMS	JUNGLE	PRIDE
BEN	EXCUSES	LIE	PRINCE
BERNARD	FLUTES	LINDA	RANCH
BIFF	FOOTBALL	LOMAN	RESTAURANT
CAR	FORSYTHE	MILLER	SALESMAN
CARDS	FREE	MORTGAGE	SEEDS
CATTLE	FRUIT	NEWENGLAND	WILLY
CHARLEY	HAPPY	NICKEL	WOMAN
COACH	HOWARD	OLIVER	WOODS
COMMISSION	INSURANCE	PEN	

CROSSWORD - Death of a Salesman

CROSSWORD CLUES - *Death of a Salesman*

ACROSS

1. Willy's oldest son
3. A man isn't a piece of ___
4. Willy's father made and sold them
8. He would probably congratulate Biff for his industriousness
12. Biff wants money from Bill Oliver for this
14. Biff took Bill Oliver's
15. Game Charley and Willy played
16. Insurance payment
18. Opposite of me
19. Transportation that helped Willy in life and to death
20. Intelligent
21. Symbol for a product or a company
22. What one usually does in a restaurant
23. Places where plays are performed
24. What one does with one's eyes
25. I realized what a ridiculous ___ my whole life has been
26. Ranch or cowboy activity
28. Monthly house payment
32. Willy's brother
33. Biff or Happy to Willy
34. The jungle is dark but full of _____
36. ___ are full of fearless characters
38. He fires Willy
40. This is no time for false ___, Willy
41. Willy wanted Bernard to give the test __ to Biff
43. Affirmative answer
44. Neither's partner
47. Actions, things one does
48. Percentage of sales as payment
49. Opposite of most
50. Makes a living; makes money
51. Feeling of depression or sadness; you have the ----

DOWN

2. Happy tries to pick her up at the restaurant
3. We're ___ and clear
5. Willy's wife
6. What Linda makes for Willy's actions
7. Willy wants to borrow money from Charley to pay for it
8. He loans Willy money
9. ___ must be paid to such a person
10. Willy's youngest son
11. He had all the wrong ___. All, all wrong
13. Ben walked into one and came out rich
17. Author
19. Ranch animals
25. Willy's last name
27. The boys left Willy there
29. Bill; Biff wants money from him
30. Bother
31. The ___ are burning, boys.
32. Charley's son
34. Willy to Biff
35. Willy is the ___ ___ Man; he can't work in NY
37. Death of a _____
39. When a deposit bottle is broken, you can't get your ___ back
40. Biff calls Willy a 'fine, troubled ___'
42. Willy wanted to plant them
45. Person with whom Willy has a brief affair in Boston
46. The salesman

CROSSWORD ANSWER KEY - *Death of a Salesman*

119

MATCHING QUIZ/WORKSHEET 1 - *Death of a Salesman*

___ 1. JAILS   A. The salesman

___ 2. MORTGAGE   B. Willy is the ___ ___ Man; he can't work in NY

___ 3. BIFF   C. Willy wants to borrow money from Charley to pay for it

___ 4. CHARLEY   D. We're ___ and clear

___ 5. PEN   E. The ___ are burning, boys.

___ 6. WILLY   F. Death of a _____

___ 7. DREAMS   G. Willy's oldest son

___ 8. BEN   H. This is no time for false ___, Willy

___ 9. SALESMAN   I. He had all the wrong ___. All, all wrong.

___ 10. CARDS   J. A man isn't a piece of ___

___ 11. NEW ENGLAND   K. Monthly house payment

___ 12. PRIDE   L. Charley's son

___ 13. FRUIT   M. Biff calls Willy a 'fine, troubled ___'

___ 14. PRINCE   N. I realized what a ridiculous ___ my whole life has been

___ 15. LIE   O. Willy's brother

___ 16. BERNARD   P. Game Charley and Willy played

___ 17. INSURANCE   Q. Biff took Bill Oliver's

___ 18. WOODS   R. Ranch animals

___ 19. CATTLE   S. ___ are full of fearless characters

___ 20. FREE   T. He loans Willy money

MATCHING QUIZ/WORKSHEET 2 - *Death of a Salesman*

___ 1. HAPPY   A. The ___ are burning, boys.

___ 2. BEN   B. Willy's last name

___ 3. BIFF   C. Willy's youngest son

___ 4. JAILS   D. When a deposit bottle is broken, you can't get your ___ back

___ 5. WILLY   E. The jungle is dark but full of _____

___ 6. INSURANCE   F. Ben walked into one and came out rich

___ 7. DIAMONDS   G. The salesman

___ 8. PEN   H. He loans Willy money

___ 9. JUNGLE   I. He had all the wrong ___. All, all wrong.

___ 10. CHARLEY   J. Biff wants money from Bill Oliver for this

___ 11. WOODS   K. Willy wants to borrow money from Charley to pay for it

___ 12. NICKEL   L. Monthly house payment

___ 13. ANSWERS   M. Biff took Bill Oliver's

___ 14. LOMAN   N. He fires Willy

___ 15. DREAMS   O. Willy's oldest son

___ 16. MORTGAGE   P. I realized what a ridiculous ___ my whole life has been

___ 17. LIE   Q. Willy wanted Bernard to give the test ___ to Biff

___ 18. FLUTES   R. Willy's father made and sold them

___ 19. HOWARD   S. ___ are full of fearless characters

___ 20. RANCH   T. Willy's brother

KEY: MATCHING QUIZ/WORKSHEETS - *Death of a Salesman*

Worksheet 1	Worksheet 2
1. S	1. C
2. K	2. T
3. G	3. O
4. T	4. S
5. Q	5. G
6. A	6. K
7. I	7. E
8. O	8. M
9. F	9. F
10. P	10. H
11. B	11. A
12. H	12. D
13. J	13. Q
14. M	14. B
15. N	15. I
16. L	16. L
17. C	17. P
18. E	18. R
19. R	19. N
20. D	20. J

JUGGLE LETTER REVIEW GAME CLUE SHEET - *Death of a Salesman*

SCRAMBLED	WORD	CLUE
EUIRPMM	PREMIUM	Insurance payment
RAECNIUNS	INSURANCE	Willy wants to borrow money from Charley to pay for it
MAONL	LOMAN	Willy's last name
NBDREAR	BERNARD	Charley's son
RSDCA	CARDS	Game Charley and Willy played
NPE	PEN	Biff took Bill Oliver's
ARCHN	RANCH	Biff wants money from Bill Oliver for this
ELI	LIE	I realized what a ridiculous ____ my whole life has been
RITUF	FRUIT	A man isn't a piece of _____
ENB	BEN	Willy's brother
SWDOO	WOODS	The ____ are burning, boys
EEFR	FREE	We're _____ and clear
LUFEST	FLUTES	Willy's father made and sold them
RCA	CAR	Transportation that helped Willy in life and to death
EGJLUN	JUNGLE	Ben walked into one and came out rich
AMISNDDO	DIAMONDS	The jungle is dark but full of _____
CSEEXSU	EXCUSES	What Linda makes for Willy's actions
REASWSN	ANSWERS	Willy wanted Bernard to give the test ____ to Biff
YPAHP	HAPPY	Willy's youngest son
DGNWENALNE	NEWENGLAND	Willy is the ___ _____ Man; he can't work in NY
KLNECI	NICKEL	When a deposit bottle is broke, you can't get your _____ back
WAODHR	HOWARD	He fires Willy
VOELRI	OLIVER	Bill; Biff wants money from him
RESTHYFO	FORSYTHE	Happy tries to pick her up at the restaurant
ICOSOIMNSM	COMMISSION	Percentage of sales as payment
LJSAI	JAILS	____ are full of fearless characters
IFBF	BIFF	Willy's oldest son
MARESD	DREAMS	He had all the wrong ____. All, all wrong.
ALCYRHE	CHARLEY	He loans Willy money
TLAFLOOB	FOOTBALL	Biff stole one from school
NAMSLAES	SALESMAN	Death of a _____.
ACOHC	COACH	He would probably congratulate Biff for his industriousness
CENIPR	PRINCE	Biff calls Willy a 'fine, troubled ____'
LMREIL	MILLER	Author
RAHDWO	HOWARD	He fires Willy

VOCABULARY RESOURCE MATERIALS

VOCABULARY WORD SEARCH - *Death of a Salesman*

All words in this list are associated with *Death of a Salesman* with an emphasis on the vocabulary words chosen for study in the text. The words are placed backwards, forward, diagonally, up and down. The included words are listed below.

```
W T M Y H X P E S D Q Z A L E S I C D K M S S N
G M J H S N S W T T F N W G T L E N Z I P L G X
R E R R J V T O H A R P R V O K B N T H S B M W
F A N X I O U S L Y N I N S I N U A T E S P C X
Z N U T B D M T I I R R V G O D I S I I N O E T
L P P C H M E I A L T E A I N L I Z P L M T F L
M A S J O R B T N V A A M C N G I F E R V E B D
Y E C C S U A Y A O I E R I N G N D A D Y B N Y
N G R O C X S L P T U D D Y S I J D I L E N L T
S E H C N I L C L Y I S L I D S E S B F O D N L
Z U N Y U I M G L E S M L Y R S U A U I I E V Y
D M B Q K R C L F M D C I Y H O C D T D I E N W
H R P D H G I Z Y Q B P Y I U A D A N P Q C D T
Q J K Q U S K A X P N G P S L L T A I C M S L G
W N W M R E X C L L Z L N P E I C C L H G D R Q
H Y V T C R D H V Y N E M D G Y N X F G B R L Y
O V E R S T R U N G S I M A D I C T A T I O N M
```

AGITATION	DISPEL	INSINUATES	SENSUOUS
AGONIZED	ENTHRALLED	INTENT	SENTIMENT
ANXIOUSLY	FALTERS	LACONIC	SOLIDIFIED
AVIDLY	GIST	LIABLE	SOLITARY
BEFUDDLED	IDEALIST	MERCURIAL	STRIVING
CANDIDLY	IMITATED	OMINOUSLY	SUBDUED
CLINCHES	IMPLACABLY	OVERSTRUNG	COMRADESHIP
INCARNATE	RAUCOUS	DICTATION	INCIPIENT
REMISS			

VOCABULARY CROSSWORD - *Death of a Salesman*

VOCABULARY CROSSWORD CLUES - *Death of a Salesman*

ACROSS
3. To say aloud to be recorded & then written by another from the recording
8. Confused
11. Willy's brother
12. Stumbles; moves unsteadily
13. One who sees the best in things; a dreamer; not realistic
15. Main idea
16. Friendship; friendly spirit of working together
18. I realized what a ridiculous ___ my whole life has been
19. Hit; smack
20. Made strong, sturdy or stable
24. Willy wanted to plant them
26. Transportation that helped Willy in life and to death
27. Bad salesmen hear this word a lot
28. When a deposit bottle is broken, you can't get your ___ back
29. Present plural of 'to be'
30. Characterized by openness; frankly; straightforward
32. Threateningly
37. Disturbance; annoyance
38. Salesmen drive them
39. Biff took Bill Oliver's
40. Quick & changeable in temperament
41. Ben walked into one and came out rich
42. A man isn't a piece of ___
43. A salesman has to be able to put a name with a ___
44. What Linda makes for Willy's actions

DOWN
1. Willy's oldest son
2. Settles something conclusively
4. Concentrating; engrossed
5. With a worried eagerness
6. Copied mannerisms, actions, or speech
7. Not attending to duty; negligent; careless
9. Held spellbound; captivated
10. To rid one's mind of
13. In a manner showing unwillingness to make peace
14. Suffering great anguish; struggling
17. Pushed to one's emotional limits
20. Appealing to the senses
21. Personified; given a human form
22. Game Charley and Willy played
23. Happy tries to pick her up at the restaurant
25. A rip-off deal
31. Existing alone
33. Struggling; working
34. Using few words
35. Likely; at risk of experiencing something unpleasant
36. Rough-sounding; harsh; boisterous
37. Enthusiastically; with great interest

VOCABULARY CROSSWORD ANSWER KEY - *Death of a Salesman*

A completed crossword puzzle grid containing the following words: BEFUDDLED, DICTATION, BEN, FALTERS, IDEALIST, GIST, COMRADESHIP, LIE, SLAP, SOLIDIFIED, SEEDS, CAR, NICKEL, ARE, CANDIDLY, OMINOUSLY, AGITATION, CARS, PEN, MERCURIAL, JUNGLE, FRUIT, FACE, EXCUSES.

VOCABULARY WORKSHEET 1 - *Death of a Salesman*

___ 1. A state of alarm or dread
    a. Incipient   b. Avidly   c. Trepidation   d. Enthralled

___ 2. Threateningly
    a. Overemphasize   b. Raucous   c. Contemptuous   d. Ominously

___ 3. Suffering great anguish; struggling
    a. Contemptuous   b. Remiss   c. Subdued   d. Agonized

___ 4. Quick & changeable in temperament
    a. Dictation   b. Enthralled   c. Mercurial   d. Incredulously

___ 5. Using few words
    a. Intent   b. Philandering   c. Laconic   d. Solitary

___ 6. Friendship; friendly spirit of working together
    a. Subdued   b. Overstrung   c. Solidified   d. Comradeship

___ 7. Enthusiastically; with great interest
    a. Incarnate   b. Avidly   c. Solidified   d. Philandering

___ 8. Place too much importance on
    a. Dictation   b. Overemphasize   c. Liable   d. Falters

___ 9. Dishonorable; disgraceful
    a. Contemptuous   b. Overemphasize   c. Enthralled   d. Dispel

___ 10. Copied mannerisms, actions or speech
    a. Striving   b. Intent   c. Imitated   d. Ominously

___ 11. To say aloud to be recorded & then written by another from the recording
    a. Dictation   b. Gist   c. Incarnate   d. Agitation

___ 12. Characterized by openness; frankly; straightforward
    a. Enthralled   b. Dispel   c. Subdued   d. Candidly

___ 13. Disturbance; annoyance
    a. Agitation   b. Insinuates   c. Falters   d. Trepidation

___ 14. Made strong, sturdy or stable
    a. Clinches   b. Solidified   c. Sentiment   d. Subdued

___ 15. Existing alone
    a. Contemptuous   b. Mercurial   c. Solitary   d. Agitation

___ 16. Rough-sounding; harsh; boisterous
    a. Incarnate   b. Agitation   c. Raucous   d. Candidly

___ 17. Tender, romantic or nostalgic feeling
    a. Sentiment   b. Falters   c. Avidly   d. Philandering

___ 18. Held spellbound; captivated
    a. Enthralled   b. Overemphasize   c. Intent   d. Anxiously

___ 19. Becomes introduced gradually
    a. Sentiment   b. Avidly   c. Clinches   d. Insinuates

___ 20. Confused
    a. Dictation   b. Befuddled   c. Insinuates   d. Ominously

VOCABULARY WORKSHEET 2 - *Death of a Salesman*

___ 1. DICTATION   A. Suffering great anguish; struggling

___ 2. LIABLE   B. Engaging in many casual love affairs

___ 3. SUBDUED   C. Beginning to exist

___ 4. INCARNATE   D. Characterized by openness; frankly; straightforward

___ 5. INSINUATES   E. Appealing to the senses

___ 6. OMINOUSLY   F. Made less intense; toned down; softened

___ 7. AVIDLY   G. Held spellbound; captivated

___ 8. AGONIZED   H. Personified; given a human form

___ 9. RAUCOUS   I. Threateningly

___ 10. SENSUOUS   J. Becomes introduced gradually

___ 11. ENTHRALLED   K. To say aloud to be recorded & then written by another from the recording

___ 12. ANXIOUSLY   L. With a worried eagerness

___ 13. SENTIMENT   M. Rough-sounding; harsh; boisterous

___ 14. OVEREMPHASIZE   N. Main idea

___ 15. AGITATION   O. Tender, romantic or nostalgic feeling

___ 16. GIST   P. A state of alarm or dread

___ 17. CANDIDLY   Q. Disturbance; annoyance

___ 18. PHILANDERING   R. Enthusiastically; with great interest

___ 19. INCIPIENT   S. Place too much importance on

___ 20. TREPIDATION   T. Likely; at risk of experiencing something unpleasant

KEY: VOCABULARY WORKSHEETS - *Death of a Salesman*

Worksheet 1	Worksheet 2
1. C	1. K
2. D	2. T
3. D	3. F
4. C	4. H
5. C	5. J
6. D	6. I
7. B	7. R
8. B	8. A
9. A	9. M
10. C	10. E
11. A	11. G
12. D	12. L
13. A	13. O
14. B	14. S
15. C	15. Q
16. C	16. N
17. A	17. D
18. A	18. B
19. D	19. C
20. B	20. P

VOCABULARY JUGGLE LETTER REVIEW GAME CLUES - *Death of a Salesman*

SCRAMBLED	WORD	CLUE
DFDDBEULE	BEFUDDLED	Confused
NIIPTENIC	INCIPIENT	Beginning to exist
NISUESTANI	INSINUATES	Becomes introduced gradually
TFASREL	FALTERS	Stumbles; moves unsteadily
TDIANITCO	DICTATION	To say aloud to be recorded and then written by another from the recording
RUTEVGSORN	OVERSTRUNG	Pushed to one's emotional limits
SRESMI	REMISS	Not attending to duty; negligent; careless
PEIASOHMCRD	COMRADESHIP	Friendship; friendly spirit of working together
NSHELCIC	CLINCHES	Settles something conclusively
YALVDI	AVIDLY	Enthusiastically; with great interest
UYLOXNASI	ANXIOUSLY	With a worried eagerness
DUEBSUD	SUBDUED	Made less intense; toned down; softened
BALIEL	LIABLE	Likely; at risk of experiencing something unpleasant
UINMYLOOS	OMINOUSLY	Threateningly
UUSNESSO	SENSUOUS	Appealing to the senses
RALRCUEIM	MERCURIAL	Quick and changeable in temperament
EIISTLDA	IDEALIST	One who sees the best in things; a dreamer; not realistic
UUCRASO	RAUCOUS	Rough-sounding; harsh; boisterous
ENETNISTM	SENTIMENT	Tender, romantic or nostalgic feeling
DILNYDCA	CANDIDLY	Characterized by openness; frankly; straightforward
TIDAMTIE	IMITATED	Copies mannerisms, actions or speech
NTEITN	INTENT	Concentrating; engrossed
RTEADLLNHE	ENTHRALLED	Held spellbound; captivated
OCINCLA	LACONIC	Using few words
EEPVMSEIOARHZ	OVEREMPHASIZE	Place too much importance on
GENIIHLDNPRA	PHILANDERING	Engaging in many casual love affairs
MCAIALYLBP	IMPLACABLY	In a manner showing unwillingness to make peace
ETNITN	INTENT	Concentrating; engrossed
GNISIRTV	STRIVING	Struggling; working
DDEFIILOIS	SOLIDIFIED	Made strong, sturdy or stable
ULROCYSIDLUNE	INCREDULOUSLY	Unbelievingly
AETNICARN	INCARNATE	Personified; giving a human form